CROSSE AND BLACKWELL 1830–1921: A BRITISH FOOD MANUFACTURER IN LONDON'S WEST END

Nigel Jeffries with Lyn Blackmore and David Sorapure

Published by MOLA [Museum of London Archaeology]

Copyright © Crossrail Limited 2016

A CIP catalogue record for this book is available from the British Library

Crossrail Archaeology publication series designed and series-edited by Jay Carver, Marit Leenstra and Andrew Briffett

Production and design by Tracy Wellman

Reprographics by Andy Chopping

Copy editing by Wendy Sherlock

General editing by Sue Hirst/Susan M Wright

Front cover: watercolour of 20 and 21 Soho Square in 1854 by T H Shepherd
(© The Trustees of the British Museum)

Printed by Henry Ling Ltd at the Dorset Press, an ISO 14001 certified printer

MIX
Paper from
responsible sources
FSC® C013985

CONTRIBUTORS

Principal authors	**Nigel Jeffries with Lyn Blackmore and David Sorapure**
Documentary research	Nigel Jeffries, David Sorapure
Pottery	Nigel Jeffries
Glass	Lyn Blackmore
Accessioned finds	Lyn Blackmore
Graphics	Hannah Faux, Carlos Lemos
Photography	Andy Chopping, Maggie Cox
Project manager	Elaine Eastbury
Post-excavation manager	Lucy Whittingham
Editor	Sue Hirst

CONTENTS

FIGURES

TABLES

SUMMARY

This book presents the results of the archaeological investigation at 12 Goslett Yard (site code TCG09; NGR 529810 181260) and two standing building surveys at 1–15 Oxford Street/157–167 and 138–148 Charing Cross Road/1–6 Falconberg Court (GCI08; NGR 529830 181320) and 12 Sutton Row–12 Goslett Yard (TCG09; NGR 529817 181727), London WC2, City of Westminster, undertaken in 2009–10 by MOLA in advance of redevelopment by Crossrail Ltd of the Eastern Ticket Hall at Tottenham Court Road Underground Station.

The archaeological work revealed significant structural and material evidence of one of the great commercial successes of the Victorian age: the British food manufacturer Crosse and Blackwell and its operations between Soho Square and Hog Lane (after 1877, Charing Cross Road) in London's West End from 1838–1921. Through mapping and integrating the archaeological data with historical sources (in particular the surviving company records) and other resources, this book tells the story of Crosse and Blackwell in this part of London's West End before its move to Branston, Staffordshire, in 1921.

From its first acquisition at 21 Soho Square in 1838, Crosse and Blackwell quickly moved to acquire and convert property to the rear of Soho Square in George Yard, Sutton Place and Falconberg Court during the next few decades. Discoveries related to this expansion included the structural remains of the 1859 sprawling complex known as 'New Building South' in the 1868 inventory of the firm's stock: a series of floors survived that yielded thousands of glass food sauce bottle stoppers, two parallel trenches that acted as a base for a steam engine and a, later, boiler, chimney base and large cistern. The cistern contained what is probably the largest collection of pottery ever found in a single feature from an archaeological site in London, with over 13,000 pots weighing nearly three tonnes dumped here. This assemblage mostly comprised refined white earthenware jars made by the Newcastle pottery Maling as containers for Crosse and Blackwell's various jams and marmalades, but also included stoneware bottles and jars used, respectively, for corrosive liquids such as acids and vinegar or to can Crosse and Blackwell's meat extract products.

Along with discussion of the archaeological finds, we examine the history of Crosse and Blackwell's product lines, from the culinary influences behind their development to how they were canned, marketed and sold in Britain and around the world. This is considered against the historical context for food manufacturing during the Victorian and Edwardian period, looking at how changes in the retail sector, food adulteration scandals and the impact of the First World War shaped both Crosse and Blackwell and the food industry.

ACKNOWLEDGEMENTS

The authors and MOLA would like to thank Will Peters (LU Section Manager) and all staff at London Underground and Mike Curran (Site Manager) and all staff at BAM Nuttall Ltd for their cooperation and assistance during this project. The authors and MOLA would also like to thank John Brown (English Heritage Archaeological Planning Officer) and Jay Carver (Crossrail Project Archaeologist).

The below-ground archaeological investigation was supervised by Paul Thrale and Nigel Jeffries with the assistance of Valeria Boesso, Vince Gardiner, David Harrison, Richard Hewett, Antonietta Lerz, Simon Stevens, Steve Turner, Steve White and Mark Wiggins. The standing building surveys were carried out by David Sorapure and Andrew Westman with the assistance of Valeria Boesso, Emma Dwyer and Michael Tetreau. Other MOLA staff involved were Sarah Jones and Gideon Simmons (surveying) and Graham Spurr (geoarchaeology). The MOLA Senior Contracts Manager was George Dennis. Nigel Jeffries would like to thank Kristiaan De Vlamynck for information regarding the curation of Crosse and Blackwell stoneware pots in Belgium and Jeremy Smith for assistance with the Crosse and Blackwell records held at London Metropolitan Archives.

FOREWORD

David Green, Professor of Historical Geography, King's College London

Crosse and Blackwell operated one of the most successful businesses in 19th- and early 20th-century Britain. From celebrity chefs and royal endorsements to innovative technologies for producing, processing and preserving food, this extraordinary company changed the nature of food production and consumption in the modern world. The company's products, or those of its subsidiaries, could be found on the tables of British and European royalty, explorers, imperial administrators and middle-class households alike. Through its constant search for new products to excite the taste, adorn the table and fill the larder of the Victorian household, this company transformed the production, marketing and consumption of food during the 19th and 20th centuries.

Crosse and Blackwell was a thriving London company, the activities of which were deeply embedded in the physical structure of the city, but whose material remains revealed a geographical reach that crossed the nation and spanned the globe. From its early beginnings in Soho, the company expanded during the 19th century to become a world-leading food manufacturer with factories, farms and markets on several continents. The taste for novelty drove experiments with chutneys, sauces, jams and hundreds of other food products that were made, preserved, pickled and packed in its central London premises. And when its products grew too numerous and too varied to be accommodated in the original premises, it constructed new purpose-built factories and warehouses to make and store its burgeoning list of packaged foodstuffs.

In this beautifully illustrated volume, the traces of those activities are revealed with reference to the material as well as the historical record. The pots, jars, packets, tins and other assorted means of preserving and storing food, together with the structures within which production occurred, provide the framework for understanding the wider processes that transformed the food industry. Innovations in storage and preservation of food, as well as new forms of transportation, encouraged changes in the methods of production, helped to create new tastes and generated novel forms of marketing and distribution – all of which are revealed in the material record so thoroughly explored and explained in this volume. In this extraordinarily rich account of operations from its base in Soho, central London, MOLA has pieced together the material culture, the infrastructure assemblages and historical evidence of one of the greatest and best-known British food companies of the period. Food for thought and a feast for the eye, this book provides a comprehensive insight into one of the most important of London's industries and one of its most innovative firms.

CHAPTER 1

THE SITE AND HISTORY OF THE AREA

1.1 Introduction

The study area, located close to the corner of Oxford Street and Charing Cross Road in London's West End, is within the modern borough of the City of Westminster and sits at the north-eastern extent of the district of Soho. London's West End is visited by an estimated 300 million people from around the world each year and Oxford Street, with over 300 shops, is considered to be Britain's busiest street. However, until the mid 17th century this area – now famous for its shops, theatres and nightlife – was mainly open fields. Situated outside the City of London, Oxford Street and Charing Cross Road closely follow routes used from the Middle Saxon period, with Oxford Street dating to the Roman period. The 12th-century St Giles leper hospital and garden stood to the east of Charing Cross Road until its dissolution in 1539, while the medieval village of St Giles focused around its parish church to the south-east.

As part of the redevelopment by Crossrail Ltd of the Eastern Ticket Hall at Tottenham Court Road Underground Station (Fig 1), two standing

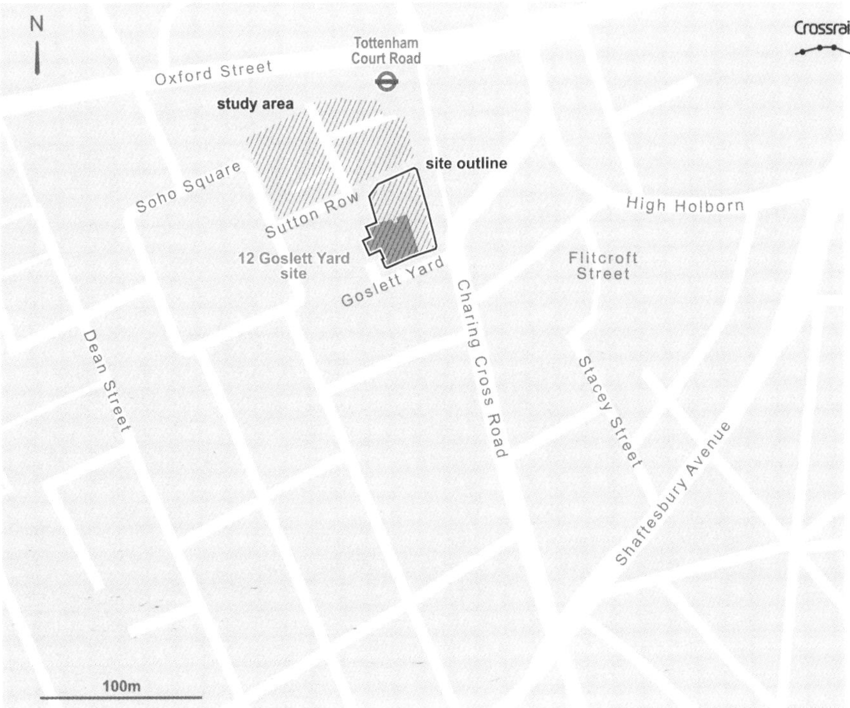

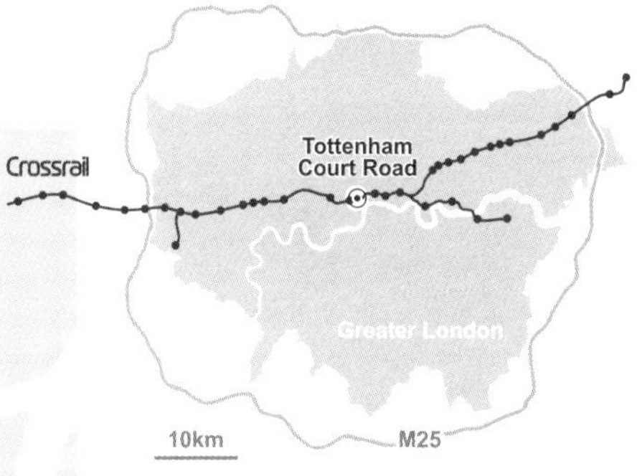

Fig 1 Map showing site location at 12 Goslett Yard and study area (scale 1:4500; inset 1:1,250,000)

Fig 2 Edmund Crosse (1804–62), top, and Thomas Blackwell (1804–79), bottom (*J S J* 1957, 13)

building surveys[1] in 2009–10 by MOLA (Museum of London Archaeology) were followed by an archaeological evaluation,[2] and then excavation, which took place in the area between June and August 2010. The site was bounded by Charing Cross Road to the east, Sutton Row to the north and Goslett Yard to the south. The full investigations revealed significant structural and material evidence of the British food manufacturing company Crosse and Blackwell and its operations in the Soho Square and Charing Cross area from 1830 until their relocation in 1921 to a former munitions factory in Branston, Burton-on-Trent in Staffordshire.

The name of Crosse and Blackwell and its foundation relates to two friends: Thomas Blackwell (1804–79) and Edmund Crosse (1804–62) (Fig 2) who went to school together and at the age of 15 were both apprenticed to West and Wyatt, a firm of salters and oilmen who had made pickles and sauces at 11 King Street in Soho (Fig 3; Fig 6) since 1706.[3] After William Wyatt made his decision to retire, the friends bought William Wyatt's business at the cost of £600[4] and on Lady Day 1830 their partnership as Crosse and Blackwell commenced trading.[5] They began their expansion in 1838 when they acquired a plot at 21 Soho Square close to King Street and built it as their main retail premises.[6] First buying and converting existing building stock and then constructing their own purpose-built premises, they soon swallowed up a large area between Soho Square and Charing Cross Road (the study area) in addition to Little Denmark Street to the east (Fig 6). Finally, they moved to Branston in 1921. It was from here that the inception and the name for its most famous product, Branston Pickle, derive.

Fig 3 Ink drawing of 11 King Street (LMA, 4467/A/03/001, 4)

By the end of the 19th century Crosse and Blackwell had become an 'incorporated' or a limited liability company (in 1892[7]) to take over the firm of the same name,[8] a move that cemented the company's position as a recognisable brand and a global enterprise that combined the roles of manufacturer, wholesaler and distributor.

In addition to the growth of the premises around Soho Square, Crosse and Blackwell became increasingly acquisitive as the Victorian period progressed, and a vinegar brewery (Fig 66) was set up by the firm between Brewery Street and Blundell Street off the Caledonian Road in 1876[9] and later extended in 1882. Here they installed one of the largest vats in the world holding 115,000 gallons[10] (522,790 litres) and thus could call upon a ready supply of vinegar that they required to preserve their products. Shortly after the First World War of 1914–18, the company obtained controlling interests in Keiller and Sons (preserves and confectionery), Cosmelli Packing Company Ltd (packers), Lazenby and Sons (pickles and sauces), Batger and Company (preserves and confectionery) and Cairns (glass jars and lids) in 1919 and 1920. Its production of jam now accounted for one fifth or one sixth of the national jam output, outstripping the remaining 400–500 jam manufacturing firms.[11] Whilst a decade after its foundation in 1830 Crosse and Blackwell had boasted a net profit of £5141 0s 6d with a stock value of £14,454 4s 1d,[12] by 1920 their capital value was £10 million.[13]

At the point it was acquired by Nestlé in 1960, Crosse and Blackwell had operated factories in the United States (Baltimore) and Canada (British Columbia) by 1910, and by 1930 it had plants in South Africa (Cape Town), Argentina (Buenos Aires), Belgium (Brussels) and France (Paris).[14] The company survives today in 2015 as a brand owned by two different food and drinks companies, Princes Ltd[15] in Europe (largely tinned soups and vegetables) and J M Smucker Company[16] in the United States (chutneys, sauces, jelly, relishes, capers, onions and mincemeat). The Branston Pickle brand and product was bought by the Japanese food company Mizkan from Princes Ltd in 2013.[17]

1.2 About this book

This book presents an account of the history of Crosse and Blackwell, as a firm (up to 1892) and then as a limited company (after 1892), and its operation in this part of London's West End from 1830 to 1921. The buildings and structural evidence of Crosse and Blackwell premises are presented (Chapter 2), before its staff (Chapter 3), products and packaging (Chapter 4), and the company's marketing, distribution networks and its commercial and global reach (Chapter 5) are discussed. The text concludes by setting Crosse and Blackwell within the context of the industrialisation of British food manufacturing in the Victorian and Edwardian era and its impact on domestic consumption (Chapter 6).

The paper and digital archives, and the finds, from the site are publicly accessible in the archive of the Museum of London, where they are held under the site code TCG09 and GCI08. They can be consulted by prior arrangement with the Archive Manager at the London Archaeological Archive and Research Centre (LAARC), Mortimer Wheeler House, 46 Eagle Wharf Road, London N1 7ED.[18]

The basic unit of reference in the site archive and below is the context number. This is a unique number given to each archaeological feature or stratum representing a single action (such as a layer, pit, ditch, etc). Context numbers appear in the text in square brackets, for example [10]. Contexts are grouped into the land-use entities referred to in this report: Buildings (B1, etc), Open Areas (OA1, etc) and Structures (S1, etc), which are generally numbered sequentially. Accession numbers given to certain artefacts are shown thus: <10>. Selected illustrated examples of ceramic vessels have been given catalogue numbers, prefixed thus: <P1>. A complete list of the catalogued pottery is given in Table 2.

The two standing building surveys were undertaken by MOLA building specialists prior to demolition by Crossrail Ltd. The first survey[19] focused on a block of buildings at 1–15 Oxford Street, 157–167 and 138–148 Charing Cross Road and 1–6 Falconberg Court, with the second[20] to the south of the site of the former Astoria Theatre on Charing Cross Road (12 Goslett Yard, 12 Sutton Row and the ground-floor shops 135a–143, 145 and 147–155 Charing Cross Road). Where possible the surveys were conducted whilst the buildings were still in use, enabling a record of the buildings, their occupants and functions to be obtained. Dimensioned sketch plans of the buildings were drawn by hand on site, together with dimensioned drawings of selected elevations, sections and other details, with sufficient information to locate them accurately in plan. Further photographs were taken by both the MOLA standing buildings and photography teams, capturing elements, structures and features that were of interest, and that helped to illustrate the change in function, layout or datable character of the buildings. This extensive archive captured the types of shops along Charing Cross Road as well as open areas and the office spaces above in 12 Goslett Yard, and in particular the unusual offices of Red Bull, occupying the top three floors of 12 Sutton Row, with glazed pod-like meeting rooms, a rooftop bar and a slide between floors.

Pottery[21] was recorded using standard MOLA codes and expansions of the codes are given at the first mention in a text section. Detailed descriptions of the building material fabrics and complete lists of the pottery codes, their expansions and date ranges are available on the MOLA website.[22] Pottery is quantified by number of sherds (SC), estimated number of vessels (ENV) and by weight (g or kg). Accessioned finds[23] were also recorded on the MOLA Oracle database. The assemblage of bulk glass (ie non-accessioned bottles, jars, lids, phials, stoppers and window glass) is large.[24] The discussion of the glass in this volume follows the typologies, terminologies (eg the various rim finishes described) and dating proposed for bottles and other forms by the historic glass bottle website.[25] The assemblage was recorded on an Excel spreadsheet using a system of codes to describe form, rim type and other attributes; numerical data comprise sherd count (SC), estimated number of vessels (ENV), weight (g) and dimensions where appropriate.

Weights and measures quoted in the text are, where appropriate, in the units used before metrication. The documentary evidence is reported with imperial measurements along with conversions. One foot (abbreviated ft) equals 0.305m. An acre is 0.4 hectare, or alternatively a hectare equals about 2.5 acres. A pound in weight (abbreviated to lb) (1lb equals 0.454kg) comprises 16 ounces (1oz equals 28g). One metric tonne equals 1000kg or 2204.6lb; 1000 tonnes or 1 kilotonne equals 2,204,600lb. One pint (or 20 fluid oz) is equivalent to 0.568 litre; 2 pints make 1 quart, 4 quarts make 1 gallon or 4.546 litres. Sums of money are quoted in the text as cited in £, s and d, where 12 pence (d) made one shilling (s) and 20 shillings (or 240d) a pound (£), since modern equivalents would be misleading. Properties of Crosse and Blackwell within the study area are discussed as buildings A, B and so on (thus distinguishable from the land-use Building sequence). County names in the text refer to historic counties.

1.3 The history of the area in the late 17th and 18th centuries

By the late 17th century, William Morgan's London map of 1682 (Fig 4)[26] shows that urban development had extended to this area as a part of the expansion of London after the restoration of King Charles II in 1660. Whilst today Charing Cross Road lies on an important historic line of communication from the north down to Covent Garden and the Strand, it had been known as Hog Lane until the 18th century (Fig 4), but probably changed its name to Crown Street after the establishment in 1759 of the Crown public house, which stood at its northern end. Crown Street also marked the parish boundaries between St Giles in the Fields to the east and St Anne Soho and St Mary to the west (Fig 4).

On the eastern side of Crown Street, development was characterised by narrow rows of terraced houses, with a dense network of small yards, courts and alleys behind. This was the St Giles Rookery, an area of poverty, infamy and ill-repute. In contrast, the land to the west known as Soho Fields (including what is now Soho Square) had been a single estate owned by the earls of St

Fig 4 Detail of Morgan's map of 1682 (Morgan 1682) and Rocque's map of 1746 (Rocque 1746) showing the Soho Square area with the site outline in red (scale 1:4500)

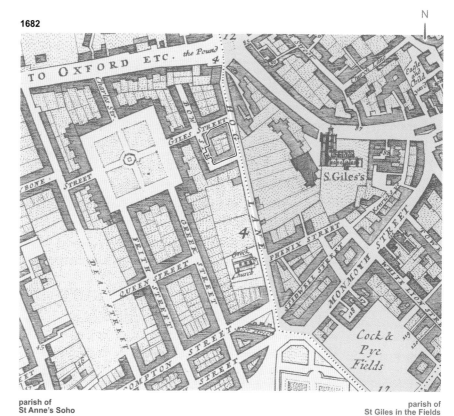

1682

parish of
St Anne's Soho

parish of
St Giles in the Fields

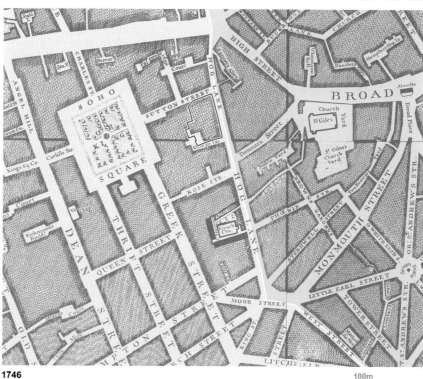

1746

100m

Albans and then Portland. Rocque's 1746 map (Fig 4) shows its mid 18th-century urban expansion was typical of the speculative development of similar estates around London at this time, with streets laid out in a regular manner with Soho Square as a central feature. The streets were generally wider and the houses were of better quality than those of the St Giles Rookery. Prior to Crosse and Blackwell's move into these premises, residents of what was to become Crosse and Blackwell's premises at Soho Square included the Falconberg family at property 20, and Lady Cornelys who lived at property 21 and who held notable masques and balls in the 18th century.[27]

A brief description of Soho from 1798 is given by a young clerk named Christopher in a letter to his parents, who had begun working for a 'Mr W____' (William Wyatt) pickle manufacturer at 11 King Street, Soho.[28] Christopher had been sent to deliver lemon pickle to the Downing Street home of the Prime Minister Mr Pitt. After describing the ruffians on his return journey from Charing Cross to Leicester Fields (now Leicester Square), he gives his parents the following description:

> Soho is a pleasant place with many great houses, but some of 'em empty since many great people have built houses nearer to Hyde Park and in ye small streets are many forayners, for ye most part French Hewgonoes, silversmiths and craftsmen, decent honest people they seem. There are many painters in Soho and writers.

During the 17th and 18th centuries, Soho and St Giles were predominantly residential but greatly contrasting in character. St Giles was notoriously overcrowded, squalid and poor. However, the population in Soho continued to increase steadily into the 19th century, resulting in the area eventually becoming one of the poorest parts of London.

Notes to Chapter 1

1 Westman 2009; Sorapure 2010
2 Bowsher 2014
3 *J S J* 1957, 12–14
4 LMA, 4467/E/01/006, 2
5 A process detailed in LMA, 4467/A/01/001
6 LMA, 4467/E/01/005, 6
7 *The Times*, [obituary of Thomas Francis Blackwell], 15 July 1907, 7
8 LMA, 4467/G/03/003/A, 15, newspaper cutting from *Leeds Evening Post*
9 Cherry and Pevsner 1998
10 *GLIAS* 1984
11 Grant 1922, 491
12 LMA, 4467/B/02/001
13 Atkins 2013, 51
14 LMA, 4467/E/01/005, 8
15 *Crosse and Blackwell*
16 *About us [Crosse and Blackwell]*
17 *Our brands*
18 LAARC http://www.museumof London.org.uk/laarc
19 Westman 2009
20 Sorapure 2010
21 Jeffries 2014
22 MOLA http://www.mola.org.uk/resource-library
23 Blackmore 2014
24 Blackmore and Jeffries 2014
25 Historic glass bottle identification and information website www.sha.org/bottle
26 Morgan 1682
27 Sheppard 1966, 73–9
28 LMA, 4467/A/03/001, 5–6

CHAPTER 2

CROSSE AND BLACKWELL'S PREMISES IN LONDON'S WEST END (1830–1921)

The firm of Crosse and Blackwell began at 11 King Street, Soho, in 1830 when Thomas Blackwell and Edmund Crosse took over the pickle manufacturing business of Messers West and Wyatt (Chapter 1.1). The King Street site (Fig 6) eventually closed in 1861, by which time the firm had progressively expanded with a complex of buildings in the Soho and St Giles areas. The first of these expansions was to 21 Soho Square in 1838–40 (below, 2.1) which had previously been two houses, converted to one and the former home of Lady Cornelys (Chapter 1.3). The extent to which the building was initially modified is unclear, but the selection of a grand house in Soho Square is interesting.

Soho was once an elegant area, with large London homes for minor gentry set within wide streets. A gradual change in the resident population took place in the late 18th to 19th century as the wealthy moved west and the desirability and value of property consequently fell, resulting in comparatively large properties being filled by an influx of Huguenot craftsmen, artists and writers, as described by the clerk Christopher in 1798 (Chapter 1.3). Throughout Crosse and Blackwell's expansion into the Soho and Charing Cross area, the firm's buildings were situated adjacent to properties occupied by craftsmen, manufacturers, tradesmen and merchants. There was little or no regulation as to the siting of industrial and manufacturing buildings in densely populated areas. As was common throughout 19th-century London, the busy streets around Soho, where the Crosse and Blackwell factory developed, were not only occupied by domestic housing, but filled with what are today referred to as small businesses.

2.1 The first expansion of Crosse and Blackwell into Soho (1838–76)

The 1850s and 60s were a period of great expansion for the firm, which followed a pattern of acquisition and the conversion of existing building stock located between Soho Square and Crown Street (after 1877, Charing Cross Road), in particular in George Yard, Sutton Place, Sutton Street and

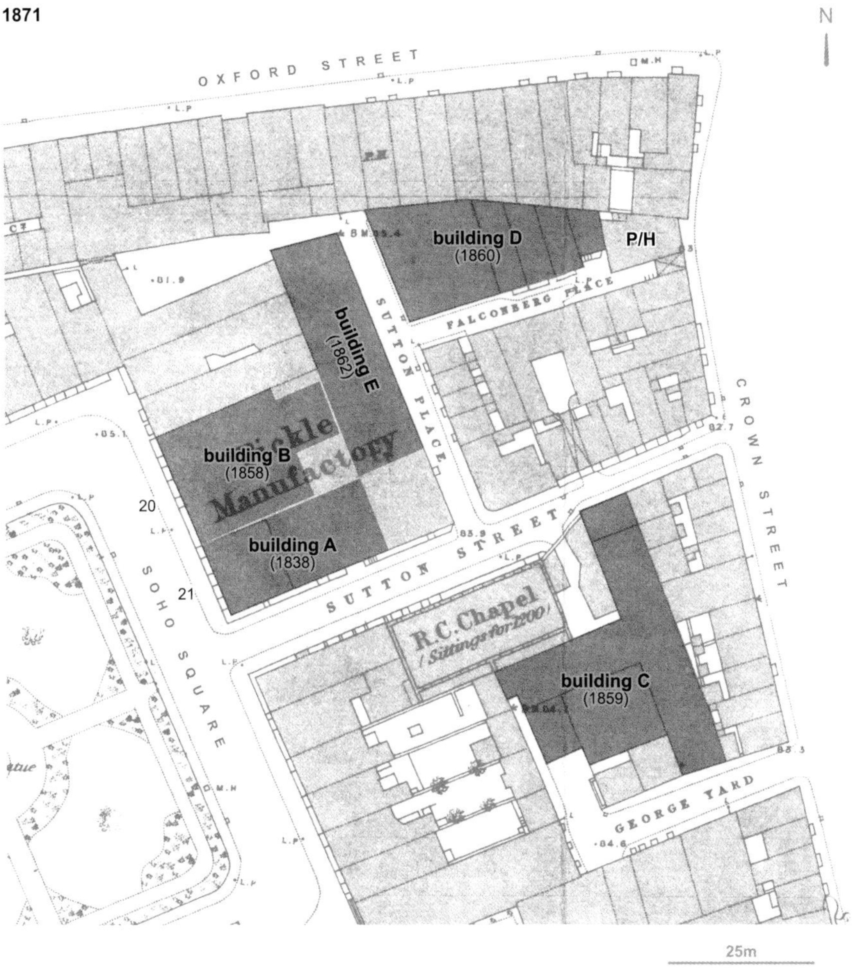

Fig 5 Plan of buildings A–E superimposed on the 1871 Ordnance Survey map (scale 1:1250)

Falconberg Court or Place (Fig 5; buildings A, B, D and E) and the construction of a large warehouse in 1859 (Fig 5; building C), referred to in 1868 as 'New Building South'.[1]

During the same period, they also acquired other outlying buildings in the West End: first at 77 Dean Street (1840), then 4 Little Denmark Street (1851) and finally the Stacey Street premises (Fig 6). These provided a range of additional functions and capabilities to complement their Soho Square operation, with Dean Street, a three-storey building and one-time home to the French ambassador, used as stables and, by at least 1878, also home to their tin department.[2] Little Denmark Street, a two-storey building with a basement and yard area, operated as their main site for the production, containing and warehousing of fruit-based products such as jams, preserves and confectionery.[3]

The exact date of the company's acquisition of the Stacey Street site is unclear, although a date in the late 1850s to early 1860s seems probable as there

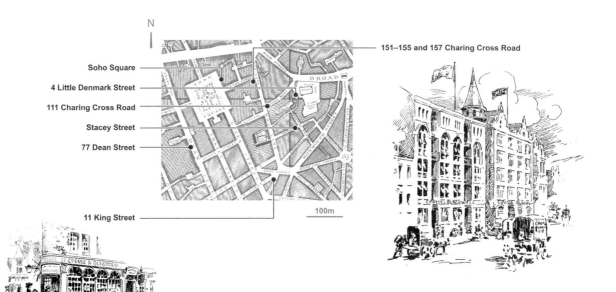

Soho Square
4 Little Denmark Street
111 Charing Cross Road
Stacey Street
77 Dean Street

151–155 and 157 Charing Cross Road

11 King Street

100m

Fig 6 Plan showing the location of Crosse and Blackwell's original and ancillary sites mentioned in the text at 11 King Street and 77 Dean Street, Stacey Street, 111, 151–155 and 157 Charing Cross Road and 4 Little Denmark Street in relation to their main Soho Square premises, superimposed on Rocque's map of 1746 (Rocque 1746) (scale 1:10,000)

(LMA, 4467/A/03/001, 4; 4467/G/03/002, 291–2)

is no listing of Crosse and Blackwell in the 1857 *Post Office London directory*. The Stacey Street property appears to have fulfilled a variety of different functions: it was a single-story premises used as either a tin-making or repair shop from at least 1868;[4] it housed the company's export pickle factory[5] from 1878; and by 1884 it had become the firm's candied peel factory.[6]

After acquiring their Soho Square premises (Fig 5; buildings A and B) the firm initially expanded to the south (Fig 5; building C) before they moved eastwards into Falconberg Court (Fig 5; building D) and to the rear of building B, into the site of a dance academy (Fig 5; building E). Building C, on the southern side of Sutton Row occupied much of the block bounded by Sutton Row to the north, George Yard to the south (now Goslett Yard) and Crown Street to the east (now Charing Cross Road), taking over buildings formerly occupied by a number of small traders. The lists in the *Post Office London directory* for 1857 describe Crosse and Blackwell's premises on the corner of Sutton Street as an Italian warehouse. The directory lists also show that in the 1850s Soho Square was occupied by a number of musical-instrument-makers, in particular pianoforte manufacturers, along with music publishers, accordion-makers, shoemakers, silk-mercers, a leather-modeller, artists, dentists and surgeons.

Prior to Crosse and Blackwell's expansion into Sutton Street in the late 1850s (Fig 5; building C), that property had been home to a number of different merchants and manufacturers. These included a tailor, picture-framer, cooper, carpenter's tool-maker, newsagent, metal-dealer, shoemaker and coach-wheel-maker. St Patrick's Roman Catholic chapel, built in the 1790s, was situated at the western end of the street (Fig 5; St Patrick's chapel still remains, though the existing building dates to 1891–3). Falconberg Court was home to the firm of William and Jasper Bailes, cabinetmakers.[7]

In 1857 George Yard, to the south, was also home to a number of diverse businesses and occupants including the London Fire Engine Station Number 9, a hot-presser, a fringe-maker, a carver and guilder, a coach-maker, plus the firm of Alfred Goslett and Company, plate glass manufacturer and merchant, from which the present street of Goslett Yard gets its name.[8]

This particular area at the centre of Crosse and Blackwell's complex, bounded by Crown Street (Charing Cross Road), Sutton Street (Sutton Row) and George Yard (Goslett Yard) was the subject of archaeological investigation and standing building survey by MOLA (Chapter 1.2). The evidence from the above and below ground archaeology clearly illustrated the development of the buildings within this area and an account of this development is given in detail below. The interpretation of this complex sequence is aided by two documents. The first is a schematic chart sequencing the firm and company's acquisitions up to 1910, which appears at the end of *A bundle of old letters 1706–1910* (Fig 7).[9] The second is a lengthy handwritten inventory of 1868 of the firm's possessions, with the following lengthy title: 'An inventory & valuation of the plant, utensils, fixtures and sundry effects on the premises at Soho Square, Sutton Place, George Yard, Little Denmark Street, Stacey Street, Dean Street and Earl Street. The property of Messers Crosse and Blackwell, made & taken as on the 1st January 1868.'[10] Unfortunately, if ever there had been an accompanying map or plan showing the various buildings described

Fig 7 Schematic chart showing the sequence and date of acquisition for Crosse and Blackwell's different premises (LMA, 4467/A/03/001, end page)

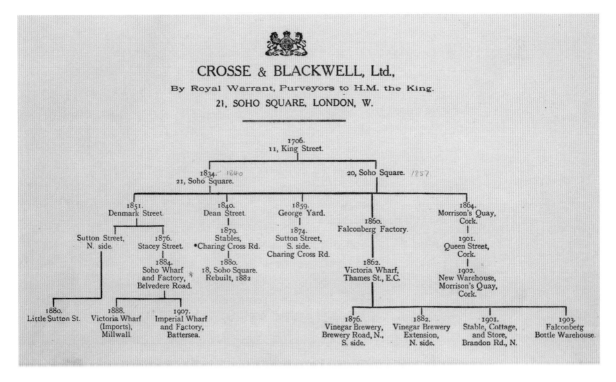

it has been separated from the text and lost, but the surviving part gives a good impression of the company's size, indicating the location of sites of manufacture during this period of expansion.

For the main site, including the Soho Square buildings, Sutton Place and George Yard, the premises are described together in the inventory, but outlying sites are described individually. Though the precise activities undertaken in these sites are not always presented, the functions of the buildings can be interpreted from the description of the contents. The following is a summary of the descriptions of these outlying buildings given in the 1868 inventory,[11] with our comments as to the likely function of the buildings; where possible, known numbered addresses are given, but for some of their premises only the headings and street/yard locations provided in the 1868 inventory are available.

21 Soho Square, 1838 (building A)

As we have seen, 21 Soho Square (building A, Fig 5; Fig 8) was the first building occupied by Crosse and Blackwell in 1838 on what was to become their central factory complex. In 1840 the firm began the manufacture of fruit preserves from a factory at the rear of 21 Soho Square. In a letter to his brother dated July 1840 a visitor to the factory described Mr C____ (presumably Mr Crosse), as 'A most amiable Gentleman'. He goes on to say: 'He went with me all over the great works and shewed me the department at the back … where they are already beginning the work of preserving the summer's fruit. It is droll how the smell of fruit pervades everywhere.'[12]

20 Soho Square, 1858, demolished 1924 (building B)

Crosse and Blackwell acquired 20 Soho Square in 1858 (building B; Fig 5; Fig 8; Fig 10). This had been a large, grand house, the Falconberg family's London residence, with the facade remodelled by Robert Adam in the 1770s.[13] The building's facade had ashlar blocks at ground-floor level, with pilasters rising from first-floor level to the cornice, topped by a balustrade at the roofline. Despite its grand 18th-century appearance, 20 Soho Square was adapted by Crosse and Blackwell to provide office space, bottling rooms and, initially, the export labelling department (Fig 9). By 1840 the firm had established stables in Dean Street, Soho (above), at the back of a large house, formerly the residence of the French ambassador, and with these horses wagons of produce (Fig 31) were brought into Soho. This seems out of keeping with Soho Square as it is today, but in the 1850s live cattle were kept in cowsheds at the rear of 20 to provide fresh milk for recipes, along with the occasional early morning drink for workers. Later in the 1870s, the firm moved the stables to larger premises at 111 Charing Cross Road (below, 2.2; Fig 21).[14]

CROSSE AND BLACKWELL'S PREMISES IN LONDON'S WEST END (1830–1921)

By the time of the 1868 inventory,[15] this site had expanded with a substantial building or buildings at the rear (Fig 5; building E; below), accessible from Sutton Place to the east. Though 20 has a separate entry of its own, it appears that 21 and the buildings to the rear are treated as one, as the 1868 inventory lists an intriguing multitude of different functions and spaces (listing them A–I, with the entries related to 20 Soho Square as A–D), with what may be a shop or showroom, along with offices for the export counting house, a private residence (probably for a resident employee), but notably rooms for specific products – with a meat, bacon and spices room (eg cayenne room) all listed. An abbreviated version of the 1868 entry is as follows.

20 SOHO SQUARE (areas A–D and J–O on 1868 inventory)

A – cellars under shop
- slate oil tanks – total 5815 gallons (26,435.0 litres)
- tank room – steam coils with swan necks
- cheese store
- pickling vault – slate pickling tank

Fig 10 Watercolour of 20 and 21 Soho Square in 1854 by T H Shepherd (Sheppard 1966, pl 92)
(© The Trustees of the British Museum)

CROSSE AND BLACKWELL 1830–1921

B – shop
- windows, shelved, roller blinds, mahogany counter, dwarf partitions
- shop counting house – dwarf partitions, desks, book rack, umbrella stand, letter scales, weights, map of London
- right-hand side of shop – drawers, shelves, writing slope
- strong room – iron shelves, two safes, 11 japanned boxes
- end of shop – glass panelled enclosure, desks, writing slope
- left-hand side of shop – washstand, counters, desks, eight-day dial
- lavatory
- outside building royal arms over shop and panelled lettered sign board

C – export counting house
- desks, files, shelves, racks, etc
- lavatory
- country office – mahogany desks, maps, hat pegs, japanned boxes
- furniture (in private residence), landing, kitchen, dining room – includes cups, tea trays, etc – presumably company property
- landing outside country office – wash sink, hat pegs, glazed stair enclosure
- meat room and adjoining landing – fat pots, gas heaters, bins, shelving, benches
- cayenne room – shelving, bins
- bacon room – shelving, benches, meat-filling machine fixed to bench
- warehouse over back of shops – crab crane, iron jib outside building, bins, shelving

D – tinman's shop
- front shop – work benches
- upper tinman's shop – press machine for stamping out ironwork, fixed to stand; four rollers, guillotine, sliding gauge, soldering irons
- lock-up store – cutters, punches of various shapes and sizes

The 1868 inventory supplies a description of the items on each floor of 20 Soho Square.[16] Although the Goad insurance map (Fig 20),[17] dates from 1889, 18 years after the compilation of the 1868 inventory, some features listed in the inventory, such as the three boilers in the ground-floor boiler room, can be identified. The inventory continues the list using letters J to O and includes the following:

J – ground floor
- counting house, office

K – lock-up
- filled with bins, cupboards, shelves, glazed 'shew [show]' cases, zinc lining for bins, weighing machines
- painting room – counters, bins, pails, brushes, tins of paint

L – boiler house
- gangways over boilers, ladders, coal waggon, coal hammer/axe
- three wrought iron Cornish steam boilers, 22ft, 30ft and 18ft (6.7m, 9.2m and 5.5m respectively) long, valves, tubes, gauges, etc

- cast iron hot water cistern

M – no. 20, first floor
- bottle room – bins, shelves, enclosures, 14 chairs, writing desk
- vase room – iron moulds
- private office/counting house – 'shew [show]' case, mahogany desk
- lavatory

N – no. 20, second floor
- essence room – bins, shelves, showcases, speaking tubes
- paper room – fitting up bins, etc
- new warehouse – cloak room, lift, washing trough, steam pans, three labelling brushes and jars

O – no. 20, top floor
- lock-up – bins, shelves, lifting apparatus
- mustard room and room adjoining – copper melting pot, bins, counters
- spice room
- honey room
- new kitchen; lead lining on floor, hoist, office, steaming tubs, steam pans, cisterns, wrought iron steam cooking apparatus, 23 galvanised iron frames for jelly bags
- kitchen lock-up – shelves, bins
- scullery

The building was retained as offices by Crosse and Blackwell after they had moved production out of Soho to Branston in 1921. However, 20 Soho Square was demolished in 1924 and replaced with a new eight-storey office building which Crosse and Blackwell occupied into the 1960s.[18] As a result of the company's takeover by Nestlé, its functions moved to their headquarters in Croydon (Surrey) by 1969.[19]

Sutton Street and George Yard: New Building South, 1859, remodelled 1877–85, demolished 1922 (building C)

In 1859 the firm first established itself on the southern side of Sutton Street in a building (Fig 5; building C) that sat within the block bounded by George Yard to the south, Crown Street (later Charing Cross Road) to the east and Sutton Street (later Sutton Row) to the north. The 1868 inventory describes this as the 'New Building South' and it was formed by a long north–south building, with a branch running to the west.[20] It sat within the centre of the block, separated from Crown Street by a row of properties and was accessed from the north via a small yard off Sutton Street, with further access likely from George Yard to the south.

Both the below-ground archaeology and the standing buildings within this particular part of the Crosse and Blackwell complex were investigated by MOLA. The second building recording survey[21] and the excavations revealed a direct link between the upstanding surviving buildings and the below-ground archaeological deposits, which had been occupied, demolished and rebuilt by Crosse and Blackwell.

The archaeological deposits indicated that, in its earliest phases, the area had been open ground followed by an episode where the site had been levelled to allow for the construction of the earliest buildings, which date to the late 17th to early 18th century. As shown on the 1682 Morgan map (Fig 4) the 17th-century street pattern was different, with a block of buildings bounded by Hog Lane to the east, Giles Street (later Sutton Street) to the north and Bow Street to the south and west. Bow Street would later be blocked by buildings to form George Yard, but the excavations in this area identified a series of four 17th- to 18th-century properties facing west on to Bow Street (Fig 11, B1–B4).

The northern two properties (B1 and B2, Fig 11) were basemented and the northernmost had a brick-floored cellar with a vaulted alcove. However, by the mid 18th century they were remodelled and extended west (Fig 12, B5 and B6), thus blocking Bow Street, and George Yard was formed. In the late 18th to early 19th century a set of steps (S4, Fig 12) were constructed joining the cellar basements of Buildings 5 and 6. The extension and joining together

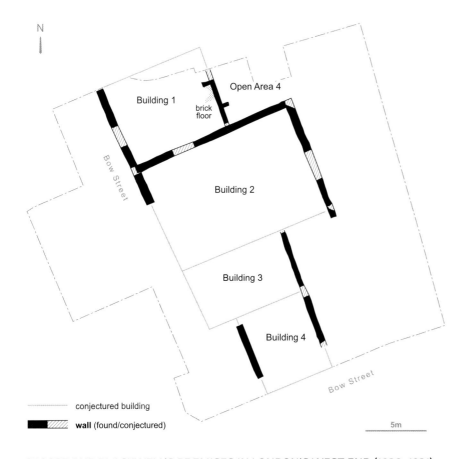

N

Building 1

Open Area 4

brick
floor

Bow Street

Building 2

Building 3

Building 4

Bow Street

conjectured building

wall (found/conjectured)

5m

Fig 11 The excavated footprint of four 17th- to 18th-century properties (B1–B4) facing west on to Bow Street (scale 1:300)

of these buildings at basement level is interesting as it is suggestive of the changing nature of the area at this time. The two original residential houses make way for a combined property, probably with a light industrial purpose. To the south, Buildings 3 and 4 (Fig 12) on the corner of George Yard were demolished and rebuilt as three properties (B10–B12, Fig 13) at this time and along similar boundaries. However, a small alleyway (OA5, Fig 13), running west to east between Buildings 10 and 11, was also constructed which drained with a circular soakaway (S10, Fig 13).

The two properties to the south (B11 and B12, Fig 13), however, were to remain outside of the occupancy of Crosse and Blackwell when in 1859 the firm acquired its first building in this block, which included the three northernmost buildings (B8–B10, Fig 13) of George Yard. This is almost certainly the New Building South (building C; Fig 5) described in the 1868 inventory.[22] The exact form and appearance of the building they acquired is uncertain, but its shape in plan appears complex, with a long north–south element, set back and with no access from Crown Street to the east (now Charing Cross Road). An arm of the same building (B8) extended westwards; this was the late 18th-century property with the brick basement that had been extended west blocking off the former Bow Street, along with the building to the south (B9; Fig 13).

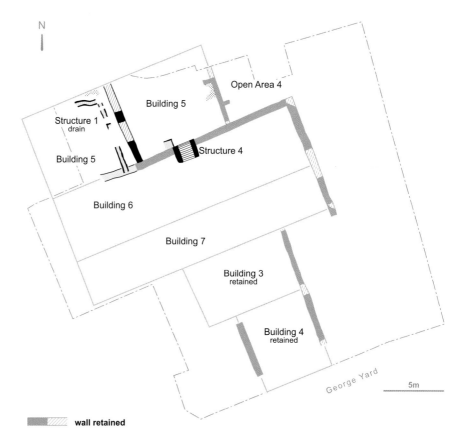

Fig 12 Mid–late 18th- to early 19th-century alterations to Buildings 5 and 6 within the New Building South area (scale 1:300)

The sprawling nature of the building in plan was perhaps the result of it being formed by a number of separate buildings being merged together, a pattern familiar in the early expansion into Soho Square and Falconberg Court.

The description given in the 1868 inventory for New Building South reflects this disjointed aspect. It is somewhat confusingly spread out and jumps from the second floor of one building to the cellars of another. As far as can be ascertained, the information given for New Building South is as follows.

NEW BUILDING SOUTH (Sutton Place [Street]; building C, Fig 5)

cellars
- loading pulley, bins, trucks, hooks, chains

ground floor
- caper room – shelves, bins, workshop
- machine room – seven horsepower steam engine, A-frame, shafting, bearings, riggers, drive shafts (to power) – two coffee mills, anchovy mill, anchovy mixing machine, meat chopping machine, iron plunger pump, mixing machine, meat mills
- engineer's shop next to machine room
- yards and landing – notice boards
- WC, tubs, steam engine, lift

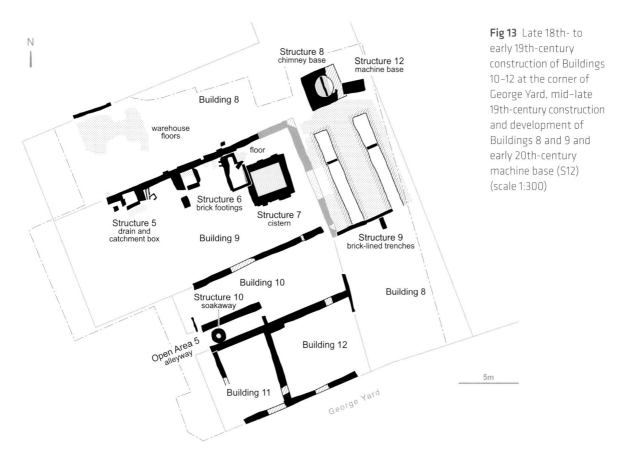

Fig 13 Late 18th- to early 19th-century construction of Buildings 10–12 at the corner of George Yard, mid–late 19th-century construction and development of Buildings 8 and 9 and early 20th-century machine base (S12) (scale 1:300)

first floor
- single purchase crane
- country warehouse no. 1 – Indian rubber spring on doors, bins, shelves, staircase

second floor (jam room adjoining)
- country warehouse no. 2
- confectionery pans, tubs, bins

cellars under dry goods store
- dry goods store
- country warehouse
- jam room

third floor
- confectionery north

In addition, the New Building South is identifiable to the George Yard area comprising a bottle washing facility.

NEW BUILDING SOUTH (George Yard, building C, Fig 5)

bottle washing place
- four butts, water mains
- single purchase crane
- sieves, iron pans, water supply
- stables

The location of the following 1868 inventory[23] entries are less certain and may be within the north end of New Building South on the southern side of Sutton Street, though a position on the north side of Sutton Street, adjoining the rear of the Soho Square buildings is also a strong possibility. The mention of a cooperage is worthy of note as on the Goad insurance map of 1889 this activity was certainly undertaken in the remodelled and surviving western arm of New Building South (building C) (Fig 20; discussed further below).[24]

NEW BUILDING SOUTH (Sutton Place; building C, Fig 5)

- cooperage
- smith's shop and forges
- dry cask warehouse
- cooper's shop
- basketmaker's room

The mention of the seven horsepower steam engine under the Sutton Place heading is of interest. Boilers are described in the entry for 20 Soho Square, but the steam engine is a significant feature, not observed anywhere else in the 1868 inventory.[25] Via a series of cranks and drive shafts the steam engine would have powered a number of different milling machines, a common arrangement in 19th- and early 20th-century factories. It is clear that in 1868 New Building South was a warehouse and factory building and a centre for the milling of ingredients on the ground floor, with confectionery and jam making, along with warehousing on the floors above. By 1889, however, the Goad insurance map (Fig 20) shows the northern part of the building had been replaced, while food processing and manufacturing had ceased in the remaining southern part, which now housed a cooperage. However, the steam engine mentioned in the 1868 inventory may well have been of a considerable size and archaeological features that could relate to its presence were identified during excavations.

Traces of a large room (B8) constructed entirely of firebricks were found, datable to the mid to late 19th century. This room contained a circular brick-lined feature (Fig 13, S8; Fig 14) lying at the end of two long, parallel brick-lined trenches (S9; Fig 15). The circular feature may have formed part of a chimney base, or similar, while the two brick-lined trenches (S9) formed a central platform, which could be interpreted as the base for a large steam engine. Although firebricks were used, there was little evidence they were exposed to high temperatures, though soot deposits were present. This suggests that rather than a high-temperature fire within a built structure, such as a kiln or oven, the fire was contained elsewhere, perhaps within the fire-box of the steam engine. The circular feature and the brick-lined trenches also appear to go out of use at the same time, when the circular feature was halved and the trenches reduced in length and partially filled with rubble (Fig 13). This suggests a degree of down-sizing or reuse, perhaps as a result of the demolition of the northern part of New Building South in conjunction with the start of construction of Robert Lewis Roumieu's building at 151–155 Charing Cross Road in 1877 (building F; Fig 19; below, 2.2).

Fig 14 Brick-lined chimney base (S8) during excavation, looking north-east

On this point it is interesting to note the Goad insurance map of 1889 (Fig 20), produced some 12 years after the northern part of New Building South was demolished. It presents Roumieu's new building for Crosse and Blackwell at 151–155 Charing Cross Road (begun 1877, completed by 1885: Fig 19, building F), with the surviving part of New Building South adjacent and to the south. The hashed symbol for a large brick-lined boiler base is represented in the spot corresponding to the site of the brick-lined trenches found during excavations, along with a square containing an angled cross to its north, which indicates the presence of a factory chimney (a further small boiler base is shown to the south, but this was beyond the limit of excavations) (cf Fig 13; Fig 20). It is certainly possible that the steam engine mentioned in 1868 had been removed and replaced by a boiler, its base reduced in size and its chimney adapted by the time of the noted Goad insurance map.

In addition to the firebricks, chimney base (S8) and the brick-lined trenches (S9), the excavations revealed evidence for warehouse features relating to Crosse and Blackwell, which showed their use, alteration or abandonment over time. Within Building 9 a large brick-built cistern (S7; Fig 13; Fig 16; Fig 17) lined

Fig 15 Two brick-lined trenches (S9) forming the central platform for the base for the steam engine, looking north-east

CROSSE AND BLACKWELL 1830–1921

with cement render and served by a one-inflow pipe was discovered. This is likely to have provided the large volumes of clean water required for this portion of New Building South. It had been backfilled, [19], [131], [149], with a large amount of pottery and glass dated 1872 or later (below). The former comprises over 13,000 vessels (48,900 SC) or 2.9 tonnes of Crosse and Blackwell's stock of pottery (Fig 17). The cistern was most likely to have been closed and filled in advance of works required for the noted construction in 1877 of 151–155 Charing Cross Road (completed by 1885: building F, Fig 19). The pots were discarded in an intact and therefore useable state. They were clean – none displayed signs of being filled with a Crosse and Blackwell food product –although some were stoppered and some had their paper labels affixed suggesting they had passed through the firm's labelling department at 20 Soho Square (above). The majority of the pots are refined white earthenwares (REFW) (<P31>, Fig 44) made by the Maling pottery of Newcastle (Northumberland), who were used by Crosse and Blackwell to supply containers for their potted meats (<P23> and <P24>, Fig 41), jam (<P35>–<P38>, Fig 45) and marmalade ranges (<P39>, Fig 45). The correlation and relationship in the dates of the construction of Roumieu's new building and the abandonment of the cistern is offered by the number of Keiller's marmalade jars here that carry their ubiquitous black transfer-printed label that advertises their awards of the London (1869) and Vienna (1872) medals. In addition, the bulk of the English

Fig 16 Cistern (S7) prior to excavation, looking north-east

Fig 17 The cistern's (S7) contents revealed: assemblage of Crosse and Blackwell's ceramic and glass stock, looking south-west

stoneware, either brown salt-glazed stoneware (ENGS) or stoneware with Bristol glaze (ENGS BRST) bung jars (<P1> and <P2>, Fig 34) and ENGS BRST upright bottles (<P4>–<P6>, Fig 34), which were also common to this feature, often present the manufacturer's stamp related to C I C Bailey's ownership (between 1865 and 1890) of west London's Fulham pothouse in Hammersmith and Fulham.[26] The glass is more fragmented, but represents some 464 items (609 SC, 16.4kg), mainly bottles (notably <122>, Fig 53; <126>) but also jars (including <134> and <135>, Fig 42), phials/essence bottles (<130>, Fig 40), 61 stoppers (including <15>, Fig 61) and five lids (including <116> and <192>, Fig 33). These assemblages are considered further in Chapter 4.2.

As noted, a large portion of the New Building South (building C; Fig 5) was demolished for the construction in 1877 of Crosse and Blackwell's new premises

CROSSE AND BLACKWELL 1830–1921

(completed by 1885: building F; Fig 19). The remaining southern and western arms were significantly remodelled and the evidence of this survived as two phases of flooring in Building 8 within the footprint of the western arm of New Building South. The later floor consisted of reused heavy iron plates resting on timber joists, which would have provided a hard-wearing surface. The iron plates are likely to have originated from a previous industrial use, possibly associated with the firebrick structures found to the east. Underlying this were related levelling deposits, one of which, [36], mainly comprised Crosse and Blackwell glass and ceramic food vessels, and the majority of the tin lids (Chapter 4.1) dating to the first decades of the 20th century. This was by far the largest single group of glass from the site, totalling some 4530 items (460 SC, *c* 85kg), of which 4294 are stoppers, including <77> (Fig 54), <98> (Fig 56), <57>, <72>, <74>, <79>, <82>, <84> (Fig 62), <71> and <76> (Fig 63), and 29 are lids, including <112>–<114>, <116>, <189>, <191> and <192> (Fig 33); the remainder are mainly bottles (<121>, Fig 53; <120> Fig 52; <124>) and jars, with a few phials/essence bottles. Beneath this were the remains of a timber floor of softwood planks, resting on joists, representing an earlier warehouse floor, the initial floor of New Building South (building C; Fig 5).

Further evidence of the remodelled western arm of New Building South (1877–85) survived to the south within Building 9. Here a brick-lined drain with a drain catchment box for a downpipe (S5; Fig 13) and two brick-built footings (S6; Fig 13) and floor were added, probably to coincide with the laying of the last phase of flooring to the north. Both Structure 5 and Structure 6 post-date the disuse of the cistern (S7) and are likely to be part of the cooperage marked on the Goad insurance map (Fig 20) of 1889.

In the north-east area of the site and still just within the footprint of the southern half of New Building South (building C) an early 20th-century brick and concrete plinth for a base (S12) for a refrigerating machine was recorded (Fig 13; Fig 18). This included an oval brass plate on the machine base with eyes for attachment on either side (<28>, Fig 18); the lettering in relief reads 'J. & E.HALL, LD / MAKERS. / REFERENCE NO / M323 / DARTFORD, ENGLAND' on a cross-hatched background and within a flat border. J and E Hall Ltd was a company based in Dartford since 1785 as maker of foundry equipment, but which later branched into transportation (including lifts and escalators), and was a pioneer of refrigeration, supplying ships and warehouses, hospitals and hotels with cold storage facilities from the early 20th century onward. A second object related to this company is a large rectangular plaque (30 x 13mm) (<27>; Fig 18) with eyes for fixing to the wall at the midpoint of either side, and octagonal bolts that secure a separate element on the back, made of folded sheet metal and apparently designed to grip a rectangular object. The front bears the words 'J&E HALL LTD / DARTFORD' with 'B1' in the bottom right corner; at the centre of the right side is a smaller

Fig 18 Brick and concrete plinth for a machine base (S12), during excavation, with brass oval plaque <28> and rectangular plaque <27> in the foreground, looking north-east

plate (60 x 30mm), held in place by round-headed screws. The incised lettering (upside down in relation to the main panel) reads 'USE MINERAL / OIL ONLY / VACUUM DTE AA'.

In the excavated north-west area of the site, levelling deposits [34] and [43], recorded as overlying earlier warehouse floors, contained large quantities of Crosse and Blackwell pottery and glass. These related deposits yielded up to 1466 ceramic vessels (7853 SC, 291kg); like the cistern assemblage (Fig 17) these pots were also unfilled and had been cleaned. However, there remain distinct differences between the compositions of the two assemblages. Deposits [34] and [43] yielded more of the refined white earthenware (REFW) plain and straight-sided cylindrical jars (<P32>, Fig 44) and two types wholly absent from the cistern assemblage: the English stoneware with Bristol glaze (ENGS BRST) mustard jars (<P7>, Fig 34) and the refined white ware with blue transfer-printed decoration (TPW2) ginger jars (<P40> and <P41>, Fig 46). Whilst English brown salt-glazed stoneware (ENGS) and ENGS BRST bung jars remain common to both assemblages, the REFW vertically grooved marmalade and jam jars made by Maling (eg <P25>, Fig 44) and the ENGS BRST upright bottles (<P4>–<P6>, Fig 34) feature less. The various labels applied to the REFW plain and straight-sided cylindrical jars in these underfloor make-up deposits proudly advertise Crosse and Blackwell as purveyors of foods to 'His Majesty the King' and are therefore related to stock used during the reigns of either Edward VII (1901–10) or George V (1910–36) who occupied the throne during the company's latter years in Soho (until their move in 1921). A near-complete large iron spoon-shaped paddle,

<32>, originally *c* 450mm long, was also found here and is probably a piece of 19th- or 20th-century equipment used to stir the contents of a vat. The glass amounts to 333 items (509 SC, *c* 14kg), mainly bottles including <128> (Fig 48), <123>, <193> (Fig 50) and <119> (Fig 52), but also jars (<137>; and <138>, Fig 43), phials/essence bottles (<131>, Fig 40), 51 stoppers (including <102>, Fig 62) and four lids.

The context behind the deposition of these noted underfloor assemblages is related to the demolition of the southern part of New Building South (building C; Fig 5) shortly after the departure of Crosse and Blackwell in the 1920s. In its place was constructed a purpose-built, four-storey office building, built of brick infill to a structure of steel and concrete. However, its demolition was monitored by archaeologists in 2009 and 19th-century brickwork was noted on its eastern edge, suggesting a small fragment of New Building South had survived, incorporated into the new post-Crosse and Blackwell era building.

Sutton Place and Falconberg Court: Falconberg factory, 1860 (building D)

One of the final phases of Crosse and Blackwell's expansion and remodelling of existing building stock in the area occurred in 1861, with their acquisition of a plot (Fig 5, building D) that fronted both Sutton Place (to the west) and the north side of Falconberg Court. This large brick building, of five storeys with a basement and a main south-facing front, was recorded by MOLA during the first standing building survey prior to demolition. Its interior was found to have been adapted many times over the 20th century for its changing uses as commercial premises.[27] These premises are noted as the 'Falconberg Factory' (Fig 7) and can be observed on the Goad insurance map dated 1889 (Fig 20)[28] annotated with the words 'tin working', 'confectionary' and 'storage'. A high-level linking bridge or walkway can also be seen on the Goad insurance map between the western side of this building and the building at the back of 20 Soho Square (building E), spanning Sutton Place. This was the first of four such high-level walkways built of iron and set between the buildings, to allow easier communication around the fragmented Crosse and Blackwell complex. By 1903 it is referred to as the Falconberg bottle warehouse (Fig 7).

20 and 21 Soho Square: expansion to the rear of the properties, 1862 (building E)

The final phase of growth saw the acquisition of buildings at the rear of 20 Soho Square in 1862, which were accessed from Sutton Place (building E; Fig 5). The entry for building E in the 1868 inventory[29] is included in the entry for 21 Soho Square and probably corresponds to entries E–I, which relate to a ground and first-floor factory and warehouse building with cellars for oils, syrups and spirits. It was somewhere near here that the cowsheds were located in the 1850s, and from here came the supply of fresh milk enjoyed by the staff, mentioned previously, though no cowsheds are mentioned in the 1868 inventory.

E – cellars under factory
- bell-shafted soy vat 450 gallons (2045.70 litres)
- yellow liquor tubs, anchovy passing tubs, sieves

F – ground floor of factory
- crab crane and jib
- gatekeeper's office
- scales, pulleys, two cast iron steam boiling pans 150 gallons (681.90 litres) each, two cast iron steam boiling pans 100 gallons (454.60 litres) each, steam jackets, safety valves set in brickwork, oak vinegar steam boiling round gauge 250 gallons (1136.50 litres) with brick piers under piped in; platinum steam coil, vinegar slate tank, passing tubs, sieves
- Piccalilli room – sink, boiling pans, basins, hot plate with two furnace doors, brickwork flues, iron hot plate, copper raisin pots

G – first floor in factory
- enclosed counting house, passages outside office – various bins
- steam pan room – eight wrought iron steam pans, pulleys, crane, ropes, thermometers, packing benches, four bottle benches, corking machine

H – jam jar warehouse
- crane, bins, hoisting tackle from lower warehouse

I – cellars
- spirit cellar no. 1 – shelves
- spirit cellar no. 2 – funnels
- wooden spoons, two brass tapping cocks, 36 gallon (163.656 litres) earthenware cask, iron ventilator
- syrup cellar – bins, shelves
- sauce cellar – dresser boards, drawers, enclosures, bins, shelves, casks, copper melting pot
- fruit cellar – bins partitions
- oil cellar – slate oil cistern, 640 gallons (2909.440 litres), slate oil cistern 600 gallons (2727.60 litres), earthenware oil receivers
- cellars adjoining – cisterns, funnel heads from shoots above

However, a report in *The Times*, 23 May 1881, gives the following account of a fire and this building's function:

> On Friday morning a serious fire occurred at 20 and 21 Soho Square, the premises owned and occupied by Messers. Crosse and Blackwell, Italian warehousemen. The cause is unknown. A back warehouse of five floors, used as packing rooms and stores, was seriously damaged by fire and part of the roof destroyed. The adjoining warehouse and the contents were also seriously damaged.[30]

2.2 The second expansion of Crosse and Blackwell in Soho (1877–93)

Whilst the 1860s saw Crosse and Blackwell acquiring its first Thameside premises on the north bank of the River Thames at Victoria Wharf, located on Earl Street and Upper Thames Street,[31] and its salmon canning factory opened at Morrison's Quay in Ireland in 1864 (Chapter 5.2), there is no evidence to suggest their main central Soho site witnessed any further expansions. By the 1870s, however, Crosse and Blackwell embarked on a new phase and strategy of building works, which in contrast to their acquisitions of 1838–62 saw the building of new fit for purpose premises (Fig 6). The firm commissioned the architect, Robert Lewis Roumieu, who built offices and stables in 1875–6 for the administrative arm of the business at 111 Charing Cross Road, and two new warehouse and factory spaces, first at 151–155 Charing Cross Road in 1877 (building F; Fig 19; Fig 22) followed by 157 Charing Cross Road in 1893 (building H; Fig 19). These builds were undoubtedly planned to coincide and take advantage of the completion of a major new metropolitan improvement in the area – Charing Cross Road, built in 1887 – by the Metropolitan Board of Works.

Roumieu's commission at 111 Charing Cross Road was previously the site of the Plough inn, which had a large central yard surrounded by a gallery with bedrooms above and stables below; the building had become derelict. Upon acquiring the site Crosse and Blackwell demolished the Plough inn and commissioned Roumieu to build new purpose-built stables in 1875–6 (Fig 21), possibly because the 77 Dean Street stables (above, 2.1) were not large

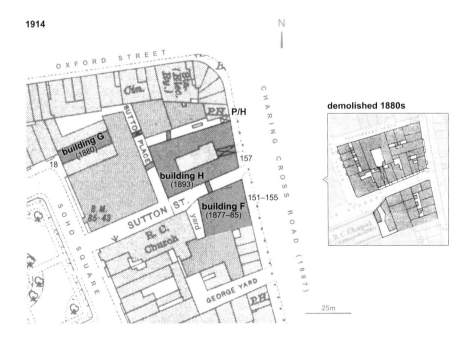

Fig 19 Plan of buildings F–H and extent of Crosse and Blackwell premises (toned) superimposed on the 1914 Ordnance Survey map; inset shows properties demolished in the 1880s featured on the 1871 Ordnance Survey map (scale 1:2000)

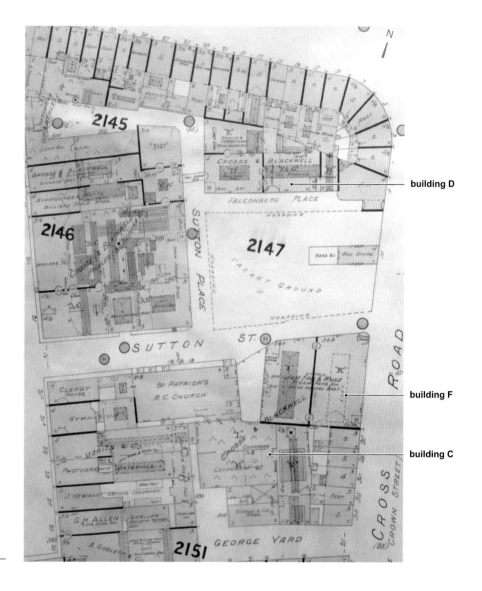

Fig 20 Goad insurance map of 1889 showing buildings occupied by Crosse and Blackwell (scale 1:1000)

(City of Westminster Archives Centre, London)

building D

building F

building C

25m

enough to cope with the increasing demands of the growing company. Roumieu's building was Romanesque in style with entrance via an archway from Crown Street. A central covered courtyard was surrounded on the ground floor by accommodation for vans and four horses. A ramp led to the first floor, where there were stalls for a further 35 horses and living quarters for the stablemen. The building remained in use by Crosse and Blackwell until their departure in 1921, whereupon it was demolished (in 1927–9) and a block of shops, showrooms and offices were built in its place.[32]

151–155 Charing Cross Road, 1877, completed 1885 (building F)

By the late 1870s further space was needed and in 1877 Crosse and Blackwell once again commissioned the architect Roumieu to design and construct a

Fig 21 Engraving of the Crosse and Blackwell stables at 111 Charing Cross Road (*Builder*, 15 April 1876, 16)
(Look and Learn/Peter Jackson Collection, XJ101705)

new building on the southern side of Sutton Street (Fig 19, building F) and marked on Goad's 1889 insurance map as a 'JAM FAC & WHSE' (Fig 20).[33] This required the demolition of the northern arm of the former New Building South (above, 2.1; Fig 5, building C; the southern part being retained), as well as the demolition of some properties facing Crown Street. The new building would therefore have a facade on to this busy thoroughfare and Roumieu, often a purveyor of distinctly French Gothic and Romanesque styles, gave this eastern facade a suitably grand appearance (Fig 22). Roumieu had built other fine examples of this style in London, including the Crystal Palace Low Level Station[34] in Bromley, and the French Protestant hospital, Victoria Park, Hackney.[35] The new building was six storeys in height with a basement and it had a distinctive turret at the north-east corner, complete with a tall conical spire, the interior of which housed a spiral staircase (Fig 22). The pairs of windows on each floor were separated by thin stone columns, while the windows of the upper two floors had rounded stone arches. Stone lintels and window sills also formed horizontal bands against panels of decorative brickwork below the windows. Internally the building was open and spacious and divided by a central spine wall running north–south. Barrels and goods were loaded and unloaded, via loading loops from the small yard to its west, accessed from Sutton Street and presented in plan on the 1889 Goad insurance map (Fig 20), while the east facade on to Crown Street had additional loading loops on each floor.

However, the new development was not without its problems. Shortly after work began Robert Roumieu died and although his son, Reginald St Aubyn Roumieu, completed the project on behalf of his father, the building work that began in 1877 was not completed until 1885. In addition, complaints about the height of the building were made as at the time it was likely to have been one of the tallest buildings of the area. It seems that the building may have been used but uncompleted until the height issue was resolved in 1885.

Fig 22 The eastern facade of 151–155 Charing Cross Road, in 1925 (after Crosse and Blackwell had vacated the premises), looking north
(LMA, London County Council Photograph Library, SC/PHL/ 01/454/WN730)

18 Soho Square, 1880 (building G)

In 1880 (Fig 7) the firm acquired 18 Soho Square (Fig 19, building G) as a showroom, but the property was somewhat separated from the remainder of the company's Soho Square buildings by 19, though linked to the Falconberg warehouse by a high-level walkway at its rear. The slightly awkward set-up can be seen on the Goad insurance map of 1889 (Fig 20),[36] with 19 between Crosse and Blackwell buildings, shown as occupied by Burroughes and Watts, billiard table warehouse. Property 18 was rebuilt or refurbished in 1882, possibly due to damage caused by the 1881 fire mentioned previously that damaged a large part of the rear of adjacent 20 and 21 Soho Square (above, 2.1).

157 Charing Cross Road, 1893 (building H)

In 1886–7, shortly after the completion of Robert Roumieu's 1877 warehouse (Fig 19, building F), the properties on the eastern side of Crown Street were demolished, the street was widened to its present width and its name was changed to Charing Cross Road. This road widening probably allowed Crosse and Blackwell to complete Roumieu's first warehouse at 151–155 Charing Cross Road to its intended height. The Goad insurance map of 1889 (Fig 20) presents the recently widened road, along with a large open plot on the northern side of Sutton Street.[37] This had been occupied by a dense block of small buildings with several internal courtyards. The trade directories indicate that this block had been previously occupied by shops, workshops and small manufacturing premises.

The firm acquired this open plot and, perhaps impressed by the continuation of his recently deceased father's work on the Sutton Street building, Crosse and Blackwell commissioned R L Roumieu's son, R A Roumieu, and his partner Alfred Aitchison to build a new warehouse, fronting Charing Cross

Fig 23 Illustration of 151–155 (far left) and 157 (centre) Charing Cross Road (date unknown) (*J S J* 1957, 16)

Road (Fig 23). The building was completed in 1893 (Fig 19, building H) and it extended west to Sutton Place completely filling the block. There was a central covered yard and a ground-floor entrance to the east on to Charing Cross Road. It was linked to R L Roumieu's building on the southern side of Sutton Street, by a fourth-floor high-level walkway, which can be seen in Fig 23. It appears that in this late phase of the development of the Crosse and Blackwell buildings a total of four such high-level walkways were used between the buildings at the rear of Soho Square, Sutton Place, Falconberg Court and Sutton Street. Little more is known about the layout of the 1893 building as it was reduced to a shell in 1926–7 when it was adapted for use as a cinema and dance hall by the architect E A Stone and subsequently became the Astoria. However, the building seems to have been intended as a warehouse, rather than as a centre of manufacturing. Its design around a central courtyard, with a vehicular entrance to the east would have allowed goods and produce, perhaps stored in large heavy barrels on one of the many floors, to be raised and lowered by crane within the central courtyard and transported either to or from horse-drawn vehicles accessing the building from Charing Cross Road.

2.3   The move to Branston

Crosse and Blackwell purchased the former machine gun factory in the small village of Branston, Burton-on-Trent in Staffordshire in 1920 (Fig 24). The factory and its accompanying offices were purpose-built for the First World War by the government, an impressive sounding complex described in the

Fig 24 Administrative building of national machine gun factory at Branston, Staffordshire, under construction in 1918; this and the associated factory buildings were bought by Crosse and Blackwell in 1920 and converted to house its pickle manufactory, where Branston Pickle was invented in 1922
(*Burton Mail*)

May–June 1920 edition of the *Square Magazine* as

seven large factory buildings which stand on 62 acres [24.8 hectares] of land, while both east and west of the factory site there are a further 90 acres [36 hectares] available for future needs. The works are bordered on three sides by the Midland, Great Northern, London and North Western, and North Staffordshire Railways, giving a siding accommodation for 300 trucks, and the whole of the buildings well skirted by well-made roads 30 feet [9.15m] wide, suitable for heavy motor traffic.[38]

Workers dwellings, modelled on a cottage design, were also built for its employees (Fig 25). Crosse and Blackwell's move to the 'garden factory'[39] model nevertheless mirrored practices employed earlier by their competitors in the food manufacturing industry, notably the jam manufacturers Hartley's, who in 1886 completed their jam factory and workers' village in the rural setting of Aintree, close to Liverpool[40] (Lancashire) following a similar venture by the confectioners Cadbury's at Bourneville King's Norton (Worcestershire) in 1878.[41]

Crosse and Blackwell began to move out of central London, though they retained offices on Soho Square, and the relocation was completed by 1921. With their departure the warehouse and factory buildings were sold off and redeveloped. The demolition of New Building South (above, 2.1; Fig 5, building C) and the construction of an office building in its place have been described. Roumieu's distinctive building (above; Fig 19, building F; Fig 22) was converted to office and showroom space, mainly for electrical goods manufacturers, in keeping with the changes undergone by the West End and Soho in particular at this time. The original timber floors were removed and replaced with steel and concrete, while the northern and eastern facades were modified to provide large window openings, with much of the original stone and brickwork either removed or covered up.

Fig 25 Illustration of Crosse and Blackwell's new workers' cottages in Branston featuring in the *Square Magazine* in 1920
(LMA, 4467/E/01/003, September 1920, 12–13)

The siting of large centres of manufacturing such as Crosse and Blackwell within central London was becoming unworkable for a number of reasons. First among these are the smells and pollution created by the location of manufacturing premises in a city like London. These are hinted at in various sources. Some take a rather romantic viewpoint: a journalist for the *Daily Graphic* newspaper reflected how 'Driving blind-folded through London there are some places that I could always recognise by their distinctive smell. One is the Oxford Street end of Charing-cross-road, where for generations Crosse and Blackwell's pickle factory has given a very distinctive pungency to the surrounding atmosphere'.[42] Others took a different view. In 1870 the Medical Officer of Health for the London Borough of Camden inspected Crosse and Blackwell's premises on Little Denmark Street following a complaint of 'suffocating effluvium' caused by the preparation of molasses for preserves, a practice stopped as a result of the visit.[43] The West End of London was once again undergoing change, with the need for office and retail space growing. This was the beginning of the West End and Soho that we might recognise today. The radical alteration of 157 Charing Cross Road (building H; Fig 23), described above (2.2), from warehouse to cinema and then to the Astoria dance hall is again illustrative of this significant change to the character and economy of the area, that to a centre of entertainment.

Notes to Chapter 2

1 LMA, 4467/F/02/004

2 LMA, 4467/F/02/004

3 LMA, 4467/A/03/001, 12; LMA, 4467/F/02/004

4 LMA, 4467/F/02/004

5 LMA, 4467/A/03/001, 8

6 LMA, 4467/A/03/001, letter to Mother from Henry H, 12 May 1884, 18–20

7 Post Office 1857

8 Ibid

9 LMA, 4467/A/03/001

10 LMA, 4467/F/02/004. The detailed description from the inventory of the riverside warehouse at Victoria Wharf on Earl Street has not been included because it is outside the study area.

11 LMA, 4467/F/02/004

12 LMA, 4467/A/03/001

13 Sheppard 1966, 73–9

14 LMA, 4467/A/03/001

15 LMA, 4467/F/02/004

16 LMA, 4467/F/02/004

17 CWAC, Goad insurance map

18 Post Office 1969, 1178

19 Post Office 1965, 1211

20 LMA, 4467/F/02/004

21 Sorapure 2010

22 LMA, 4467/F/02/004

23 LMA, 4467/F/02/004

24 CWAC, Goad insurance map

25 LMA, 4467/F/02/004

26 Green 1999, 169–76

27 Westman 2009

28 CWAC, Goad insurance map

29 LMA, 4467/F/02/004

30 *The Times*, [report], 23 May 1881, 8

31 LMA, 4467/A/03/001, 6 and 15–16 footnote 4, letter to Reginald, 26 August 1860

32 Sheppard 1966, 296–312

33 CWAC, Goad insurance map

34 Sorapure and Tetreau 2011

35 Sorapure and Karim 2014

36 CWAC, Goad insurance map

37 CWAC, Goad insurance map

38 LMA, 4467/E/01/003, *Square Mag*, May–June 1920, 11

39 Hartley 2011, 26

40 Ibid, 26–8

41 Ibid, 29

42 LMA, 4467/G/03/003/A, newspaper cutting from *Daily Graphic*, 26 February 1921

43 Board of Works for the St Giles District 1871

CHAPTER 3

CROSSE AND BLACKWELL'S STAFF

The firm's meteoric rise to being one of the largest food manufacturing companies in the world by the 1920s can be observed in the number of men and women it employed: in 1845 it employed just 15 staff at its first King Street premises, which had grown to 386 by 1865[1] and 1200 by 1881.[2] During their time in Soho from 1830 to 1921, the leadership of Crosse and Blackwell was kept largely as a family affair. Both the original founders, Thomas Blackwell and Edmund Crosse, passed on the reins to their two sons Thomas Francis Blackwell (b 1838) and Edmund Meredith Crosse (b 1846) respectively. Both founders have prominent burial monuments in All Saints churchyard, Harrow Weald, Harrow (Middlesex). Upon Thomas Francis Blackwell's death in 1907 at the age of 69, his obituary in *The Times* paints the picture of business leader, family man and philanthropist. His generous nature is noted by his giving 'freely' and 'largely' to various 'charitably institutions, schools, hospitals, and benevolent institutions'.[3] After Thomas F Blackwell's retirement in 1901 the leadership of the company was passed to his son, Samuel John Blackwell.

The company's departure from Soho and Charing Cross Road to Branston in 1921 marked the end of an era not only for the company itself but for many of its staff, for whom, according to the Chairman of Directors of the company at this time, Mr Robert Just Boyd (who had been promoted to this role in recognition of his management of Keiller and Sons), 'we cannot offer appointments in the new factories at Branston, or who, for their own reasons, do not care to leave London'.[4] This led to the dismissal of 1500 to 2000 of their London staff, employees who were recompensed with a pension if they had served over 17 years with the company, with a redundancy payout for the remainder at the cost of £22,500.[5] The relocation prompted the *Square Magazine*[6] – just one of the three staff publications that have survived (*Combine Link Magazine* and the short-lived *Soho Star*[7] are the other two) – to publish a handful of various reminiscences by staff who had served the company for decades and would have benefitted from the generous payouts it offered to these 'old and valued servants of the firm' upon the company's departure to Branston.

If Mr T Hall's reflections are anything to go by,[8] it was the tin department (then) on Dean Street[9] that offered the liveliest of workplace environments as it could only be entered by the King's Head, a 'small public house' that 'pointed the way in, and perhaps rather frequently the way out'. It was here that staff 'of the tin-shop adjourned for dominoes, push-half-penny, and in order to "take the waters". No man who is familiar with the incidents to which I refer will deny that accidents, the result of over-indulgence, were far too frequent, and the firm had to take severe measures to ensure sobriety on the premise …'.[10] Amongst the bottle glass from the site are the remains of five wine bottles, a few beer bottles and four stoppers from London breweries and a ginger beer bottle, possibly refreshments consumed on the premises.

Hall's was just one of the accounts in the *Square Magazine* that commented upon the working practices of the company prior to 1921. When he joined Crosse and Blackwell in 1878, Hall worked a 12-hour day, 'with one-and-a-half hours for meals, and five hours on Saturday',[11] an insight added to by Frank Blackwell who reminisced (in 1928) that previously, whilst it was common that clerks worked for up to 12 hours per day 'it might be anything up to eighteen hours for the factory hands'.[12] By 1919 the daily work pattern had been reduced to 11 hours per day (Fig 26).[13] Workers were marshalled by foremen, under-foremen and forewomen (Fig 27).[14]

During the summer the firm had to hire extra labour to cope with the preserves season. This task was undertaken at the Little Denmark Street premises with 400–700 extra women hired to be 'seated with the market baskets beside them, with hands well washed, and as quiet and silent as such as an assemblage of the sex could be expected to be …' (Fig 28).[15] In 1860 a commentator

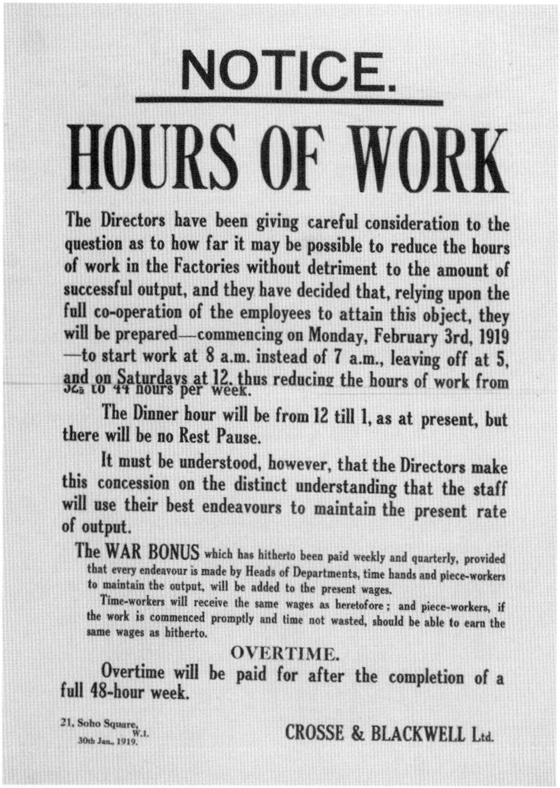

Fig 26 Poster dated 1919 informing staff of changes to working hours and practices; the reduction of workers' hours by Crosse and Blackwell followed a national trend in 1919, a year marked by significant industrial unrest in Britain
(LMA, 4467/G/03/003, 165)

NOTICE.

HOURS OF WORK

The Directors have been giving careful consideration to the question as to how far it may be possible to reduce the hours of work in the Factories without detriment to the amount of successful output, and they have decided that, relying upon the full co-operation of the employees to attain this object, they will be prepared—commencing on Monday, February 3rd, 1919—to start work at 8 a.m. instead of 7 a.m., leaving off at 5, and on Saturdays at 12, thus reducing the hours of work from 52½ to 44 hours per week.

The Dinner hour will be from 12 till 1, as at present, but there will be no Rest Pause.

It must be understood, however, that the Directors make this concession on the distinct understanding that the staff will use their best endeavours to maintain the present rate of output.

The WAR BONUS which has hitherto been paid weekly and quarterly, provided that every endeavour is made by Heads of Departments, time hands and piece-workers to maintain the output, will be added to the present wages.

Time-workers will receive the same wages as heretofore ; and piece-workers, if the work is commenced promptly and time not wasted, should be able to earn the same wages as hitherto.

OVERTIME.

Overtime will be paid for after the completion of a full 48-hour week.

21, Soho Square, W.1.
30th Jan., 1919.   CROSSE & BLACKWELL Ltd.

Fig 27 Photographs of groups of foremen and forewomen, taken in Soho Square
(LMA, 4467/E/01/003, January 1921, 22–3)

Fig 28 Newspaper
cutting from the *Daily
Graphic* (20 June 1918,
99) showing women
picking over strawberries;
note the stack of
stoneware bung jars
behind them
(LMA, 4467/G/03/003)

THE DAILY GRAPHIC, THURSDAY, JUNE 20, 1918.

Where the Strawberries are : "N.K." Food Pictures : for Fleet Street.

NOT LOST, BUT IN PROCESS OF TRANSFORMATION.
The missing strawberries have found their way to the jam factories, and expert hands are busily at work turning them into jam for the Army's needs. Girl sorters, in their white aprons, pick over the fruit before it goes into the big preserving pans. Our three pictures were taken at Messrs. Crosse and Blackwell's factory. ("Daily Graphic" photographs.)

observed, '450 women busily engaged in stripping the blackcurrants from their stalks and depositing them in the wide-mouthed bottles familiar to the housewife. … The bottles are removed, filled with spring water, turned down to drain, corked by a screw, submitted to a hot bath, cooled, and next day cellared in thousands, ready for demand at home, or foreign export, largely to our Indian Empire'.[16]

A key message frequently reinforced in the *Square Magazine* was the importance of transferring and bottling the apparent 'spirit' that permeated Soho Square and its staff to their new premises in Branston, with the thoughts of Mr V H Minton providing just one such account: 'those who had come into the business recently and who had spent most of the last year at the Square had been impressed in many ways by the splendid loyalty that permeated the whole establishment. Whether managers or representatives, they were all enamoured with a perfect beautiful loyalty. He had never seen anything like the spirit of Crosse & Blackwell, and he would like to put that on record'.[17]

In addition to publishing this gushing reflection, the *Square Magazine* frequently promoted and reminded its London workforce of the wide range of benefits Crosse and Blackwell provided. The company had not only a kindergarten attended to by teachers, a matron and various forewomen, and 'year on year the number increased until at one period we had as many as ninety-six [children]', but also a continuation school founded in 1916.[18] The *Square Magazine* boasted that the 'firm has played an extraordinary part in the education of employees since the establishment of their School'[19] and the 'provision made for instruction and welfare have always been approved and greatly appreciated by the London County Council, whose reports on the work from time to time have been recorded in the records of the firm'.[20] Similar 'continuation schools' were also run by other companies such as Debenhams, Harrods and Selfridges.[21] In addition, Crosse and Blackwell employed nurses stationed in a first-aid room to dress the cut fingers caused by the frequent handling of glass bottles in their factory on Soho Square.[22] A similar range of staff benefits were offered by Hartley's, one of Crosse and Blackwell's main competitors in jam making.[23]

The July 1920 edition of the *Square Magazine*[24] focused on how staff morale was boosted by sports days (Fig 29) held at a sports field the company appeared to own in Pinner, Harrow (Middlesex); then it was a quiet residential and semi-rural neighbourhood on the edge of north-west London, but a place where the Blackwell family had long resided and was strongly associated. Staff entered 'the usual flat races' with 'both sexes taking part' in 'egg and spoon races; throwing a cricket ball; skipping races; a most amusing obstacle race; thread-needle and interdepartmental tugs-of-war'.[25] Crosse and Blackwell also supported its hockey club which played at Pinner[26] and fielded a football, tennis and cricket team.

Whilst Crosse and Blackwell therefore provided many benefits to its London-based staff in the first two decades of the 20th century, the staff themselves had also organised a number of social clubs, for example the Girls' Dining Club opened in 1903[27] and much is made of the C&B Orchestra in the *Square Magazine*, which operated under the baton of head foremen Mr H W Bell and played various company social events during this period (Fig 30). The company's move to Branston inspired a particularly lively annual social in 1920 of the Girls' Club – just one of the many staff social clubs – as 'owing to

Fig 29 'A good finish': photograph taken at a sports ground in Pinner, north-west London
(LMA, 4467/E/01/003, July 1920, 10-12)

Fig 30 The 'C&B Orchestra': photograph taken in Soho Square (LMA, 4467/E/01/003, July 1920)

the removal of the factory from Soho Square to Branston, many of the girls will be separated, this social had a special sentiment attached to it'.[28] Held at the Portman Rooms, London 'two of the large rooms were filled with dancers from 9.30p.m. until 4 the next morning. There were three bands in attendance, and during the evening no less than 1,300 happy people were enjoying the fun'.[29]

Notes to Chapter 3

1 Atkins 2013, 45

2 Ibid, footnote 17

3 *The Times*, [obituary of Thomas Francis Blackwell], 15 July 1907, 7

4 LMA, 4467/E/01/003, *Square Mag*, September 1920, 1

5 LMA, 4467/G/03/003/A, 140, newspaper cutting from *Evening News*, 24 February 1920

6 LMA, 4467/E/01/003

7 LMA, 4467/E/01/004

8 LMA, 4467/E/01/003, The chance to make good, *Square Mag*, September 1920, 17–18

9 LMA, 4467/F/02/004

10 LMA, 4467/E/01/003, The chance to make good, *Square Mag*, September 1920, 17

11 LMA, 4467/E/01/003, The chance to make good, *Square Mag*, September 1920, 18

12 LMA, 4467/E/01/006, *Combine Link Mag*, 26 November 1928, 1–11

13 LMA, 4467/E/01/003, The chance to make good, *Square Mag*, September 1920, 18

14 LMA, 4467/E/01/003, *Square Mag*, January–March 1921, 22–4

15 LMA, 4467/G/03/003, 99, newspaper cutting from *Daily Graphic*, 20 June 1918

16 LMA, 4467/G/03/002, 162, offprint of *Leisure Hour*, 1860

17 LMA, 4467/E/01/003, Marking a record, *Square Mag*, January–March 1921, 14

18 LMA, 4467/E/01/003, Reminiscences, *Square Mag*, January–March 1921, 20

19 LMA, 4467/E/01/003, Works school, *Square Mag*, September 1920, 5

20 LMA, 4467/E/01/003, Works school, *Square Mag*, September 1920, 5

21 *The Times*, Day continuation schools, 8 January 1921, 14

22 LMA, 4467/E/01/003, First aid in the factory, *Square Mag*, May–June 1920, 8

23 Hartley 2011, 34–6

24 LMA, 4467/E/01/003, C & B sports workers have a day out, *Square Mag*, July 1920, 10–12

25 LMA, 4467/E/01/003, C & B sports workers have a day out, *Square Mag*, July 1920, 11

26 LMA, 4467/E/01/003, *Square Mag*, June 1920, 13

27 LMA, 4467/E/01/003, Reminiscences, *Square Mag*, January–March 1921, 20

28 LMA, 4467/E/01/003, Girls' annual social, *Square Mag*, January–March 1921, 23

29 LMA, 4467/E/01/003, Girls' annual social, *Square Mag*, January–March 1921, 22

CHAPTER 4

'ITALIAN WAREHOUSE AND OILMEN AND DEALERS IN PRESERVES, PICKLES AND SAUCES': CROSSE AND BLACKWELL'S PRODUCTS, THEIR CONTAINERS AND PACKAGING

4.1 The development and sourcing of Crosse and Blackwell's product lines

As the 19th century progressed, food became a subject worthy of study and discussion, and food writing became a valid pursuit and genre in its own right.[1] The development and endorsement of Crosse and Blackwell's product line of (largely) preserves, potted meats and fish (or bloaters), relishes, sauces and pickles was achieved through their regular consultations and clever use of three of the more well-known celebrity chefs and authors of the Regency and Victorian age: Signor Qualliotti, Charles Emile Francatelli (1805–76; born in London of Italian descent) and Alexis Soyer (1809–58; born in France). Both Francatelli and Soyer served as *chef de cuisine* (head chef) of the Reform Club,[2] and in Francatelli's case to Queen Victoria herself, in addition to various other premier eating establishments in London. Crosse and Blackwell continued the practice of employing a head or principal chef at its Soho/Charing Cross premises right up to the move to Branston in 1921. The head chef was tasked with overseeing the preparation and cooking of its product lines, in addition to checking the quality of the produce it received.[3]

Shortly after setting themselves up in the food industry in 1830, Edmund Crosse and Thomas Blackwell 'Italian Warehouse and Oilmen and Dealers in preserves, pickles and sauces'[4] employed the services of Signor Qualliotti, once chef to Napoleon, who came to England after Napoleon's banishment to St Helena. He introduced several new product lines – from potted meats, including Strasbourg paste (a commercial version of paté de Contades), and fish to several pickles and sauces – but his most famous legacy is the introduction of Crosse and Blackwell's Piccalilli (<P9>, Fig 35), a product marketed for Christmas 1832.[5]

The firm built on the various curry powder, relish and chutney lines inherited from West and Wyatt by taking what appears as an unusual step in sending a representative with the first troops that were shipped out to India by the East India Company. This unnamed individual sent back new spices and other ingredients for the firm to experiment with. This resulted in Crosse and Blackwell's Captain White's Oriental Pickle and Curry Powder.[6] Col Skinner's Mango Relish also appears to have been developed at this time,[7] together with Abdool Fygo's Chutney and Mulligatawny Pastes. Perhaps the most famous example of a recipe imported from India and the assimilation of foods from the subcontinent is Worcestershire Sauce. The popular story behind this product is that the chemists Lea and Perrins were asked by Lord Marcus Sandys – the former governor of Bengal (India) – to replicate the recipe of a spicy sauce that he had enjoyed whilst posted there.[8] Crosse and Blackwell later acted as a distributor for Lea and Perrins, a relationship evidenced by the glass stoppers bearing their moulded lettering which were found on the site.

Whilst Crosse and Blackwell's various Indian-inspired curry powders, relishes and chutneys chimed well with Britain's imperial pretensions and its acquisition of overseas territories as the Victorian period progressed, their relationship with Alexis Soyer and the fashionable cooking he represented aligned the firm to another important trend: French-style cuisine. This led to the firm signing a number of contracts or deed of covenants in the 1850s with Soyer,[9] which detail the agreements for the exclusive rights for Crosse and Blackwell to make and distribute his products – notably Soyer's Sauce for Ladies, Soyer's Sauce for Relish and Soyer's Relish – used in the 'seasoning of soups gravies Fish Meat and Game'. One such agreement signed with Soyer in 1853 is typical. It allowed the firm the 'sole and exclusive right of preparing and vending' of Soyer's 'Aromatic Mustard' which they would sell with his 'name and Portrait' affixed 'upon the Bottles, Jars or Pot in which the same shall be sold'.[10] The 1850s also saw the firm obtain the exclusive rights to two other product lines they had been selling and making for a period of time: 'Essence of Anchovies'[11] and 'Payne's Royal Osborne Sauce'.[12] They had been paying a commission on quantities sold to the original developers of these two products, Christopher Dinmore and George Payne (to whom they paid £40 for the rights) respectively.

The development of their lines can be observed in the few Crosse and Blackwell price lists that have survived from the 19th century.[13] That for 1846 (Fig 38)[14] has a full repertoire of products listed under the main headings for rich sauces, pickles, bottled fruit, preserves, vinegars and sundries, and sold by either weights (eg ½lb (0.227kg)) or measures (eg ½ pint (0.284 litre), quart (1.137 litre)) depending on the product. By 1860 it boasted '25 varieties of soup, over 20 kinds of crystallised fruits, many liqueurs, as well as game pates, jams and honey and similar delicacies'.[15]

Their market share can be observed in the impact they had on preserves, or the making of jam and marmalade. By 1868 it is estimated that Crosse and Blackwell supplied one quarter of the jam and marmalade consumed in London alone,[16] yet when the firm began preserving fruits early in its history at the rear of 21 Soho Square in 1840 – a decade before the recipe for jam established a 2:1 ratio of fruit to sugar, and before the acquisition of their Little Denmark Street premises in 1851 – jam represented a product whose cost was out of reach for most of Britain's population. This changed in 1870 when the duty on sugar was halved, and its abolition in 1874[17] stimulated a rapid growth in both jam and marmalade manufacturing. The subsequent reduction in price meant that jam (in particular) quickly became a national staple and it is estimated that bread and jam accounted for two in three of a poor child's meals.[18] It remained, however, a summer activity for the firm (Fig 31). Its fruits were drawn from orchards in Croydon and Orpington (Kent),[19] but after Crosse and Blackwell obtained a controlling interest in Keiller and Sons in 1918, it could also acquire the oranges and apricots supplied to their factory at Denia, near Valencia in Spain,[20] to more directly control and source the ingredients it needed to make marmalade. Fruit was preserved at Crosse and Blackwell immediately on arrival after inspection.[21]

Fig 31 Ink drawing showing fresh produce being transported into Soho Square
(LMA, 4467/A/03/001, 10)

Crosse and Blackwell's product line was underpinned by the use of contracts to tie their suppliers and the agents they employed to check the produce in the fields and arrange transport direct to London; this efficiency and system of quality control was unprecedented among their competitors.[22] They sourced their ingredients at various times from farms 'in Deptford, Greenwich and East Ham, in Kent, Bedfordshire, Cambridge and others parts of the country, of which practically the whole produce – Vegetables, Fruit, Pork, Meat and Poultry – went into the hands of Messrs. Crosse & Blackwell'.[23] During the 1860s a large proportion of the onions they pickled came from East Ham (Essex), where hundreds of women were employed in peeling.[24] The East Ham and Barking area of Essex was a very important area for market gardening which supplied London since the mid 18th century:[25] in particular potatoes but also cabbages, turnips, asparagus, onions, cucumbers, strawberries, apples, plums, rhubarb and walnuts were grown.

Some ingredients came from further afield: anchovies arrived from Leghorn, Italy, in small casks; salmon was sourced from Phillipe and Canaud of Nantes in France (the firm's contract in 1859 was worth 120,000 tins) and processed in the Crosse and Blackwell plant at Morrison's Quay, Cork, Ireland; salad oil was imported from Lucca in Italy.[26]

In the 1830s it was the noted Signor Qualliotti who obtained the meat required for Crosse and Blackwell's product line and regularly visited the 'Slaughter House' in Whitechapel, Tower Hamlets, in London's East End 'to pick up the best meat for the purpose of the new Potted Meats he has introduced which have proved a great success partly it must be through the care he bestows upon them'.[27] Buying fresh meat apparently continued into the Edwardian period, as reported in a feature on Crosse and Blackwell in *Public Health*, which records that 'fresh beef, mutton, pork and tongues and other meats are purchased daily in the market by their own buyers only after a most careful inspection, and nothing but the best is acquired. Another inspection takes place at the factory by the principal chef, and all receptacles are rigidly sterilised before the finished product is finally put up'.[28]

After the First World War, consumer tastes adapted and the *Daily Mail* reported how hot and sharp flavours were falling out of fashion, with sweet pickles, sauces and chutneys preferred; Mr W J Annis, the head chef of Crosse and Blackwell, reported how salad oils and creams and tinned fruit salad had become particularly sought after.[29]

Containers

Crosse and Blackwell products therefore required foods to be preserved in vinegar (pickles, mustards and various food sauces etc) and sugar (notably preserved fruit, jams and marmalades) which were then canned (the preservation and hermetic sealing of foods in airtight ceramic, glass or metal containers). They did not appear to practice the other methods of food preservation in their central premises, for example fermenting, smoking, salting and drying. Fulfilling their role of food manufacturer, wholesaler and distributor meant that, in addition to the regular and reliable supplies of stringently sourced ingredients, it also required large quantities of rigid containers to package items for distribution across the globe. In the mid 19th century most solid foodstuffs were packaged by a grocer in paper or card for travelling short distances and for immediate consumption. Crosse and Blackwell products, however, were from the outset of a type that required rigid hermetically sealed containers, whether glass, pottery or tin; bottles and jars for sauces, pickles, preserves and potted meats are all evidenced in the archaeological material. Glass and pottery (specifically stoneware and refined white earthenware (REFW)) were ideal materials for the food industry, being cheap to produce, impervious, inert, neutral, easy to clean and, in the case of glass, recyclable, while offering endless possibilities in shape and form, although this was to a large degree dictated by the intended contents and the necessary airtight closures, which were constantly being improved (below, 4.3; Chapter 6.1).

Whilst tins were manufactured in-house in the tin department on Dean Street, glass, ceramics and packets were obtained from a number of other British suppliers, until Crosse and Blackwell's acquisition of the glass manufacturer Alexander Cairns and the Cosmelli Packing Company Ltd in 1920.[30] This strategy had already been employed by one of Crosse and Blackwell's competitors, Hartley's, who decided that a more direct method of sourcing and controlling the production of the stoneware crocks was needed and bought the Caledonian pottery of Glasgow in 1898, adding to their existing pottery located close to their Aintree works at Melling (Lancashire).[31] Nevertheless, a regular turnover of Crosse and Blackwell's circulated stock was enabled by their returns department who received the 'thousands of empty ceramic and glass bottle and jars returned every day' for redistribution throughout its various departments.[32]

Tins

Despite the site and the noted cistern, in particular (Chapter 2.1; Fig 16; Fig 17), yielding large quantities of ceramics and glass, the excavations provided little evidence of the increasingly important material used by Crosse and Blackwell and their competitors for food canning: tins. Only 49 poorly preserved tin lids (2.487kg) of composite construction were found; the majority (44) were in one of the underfloor make-up deposits, [36] (<18>–<21>, <65>), with four in [43] (<22>–<25>), sequences associated with the demolition of the western arm of the New Building South factory (Chapter 2.1; Fig 5, building C). Only <26> was located in fill [149] of the cistern. Two lid sizes are present, with average weights of 46g (upper diameter 50mm, base 45mm; 26 examples) and 56g (upper diameter 55mm, base 50mm; 23 examples); thickness can be 10mm or 13–14mm, regardless of size.

Crosse and Blackwell had been making tins in its tin department and tin shop on Dean Street since 1840, employing up to 40 men by 1860[33] and it used tins to contain a diverse range of its products. The 1868 inventory also records how 21 Soho Square (Chapter 2.1; Fig 5) contained a tinman's shop.[34] In terms of design and technological history, canning foods in iron canisters was first patented through a London-based agent by the Frenchman Philippe de Girard in 1810, but its successful production can be credited to the British engineer Bryan Donkin who acquired Girard's patent in 1811.[35] By 1812 his diaries show he had been experimenting by cooking and sealing milk, soups and meats in tinned wrought iron canisters in a factory in Fort Place, Blue Anchor Road, in Bermondsey, London.[36] Donkin appears to have largely supplied the Royal Navy, which by 1847 had absorbed canned meats into the ship's ration.[37]

Yet canned food remained an expensive product and difficult to open – the cans were soldered shut – until the tin opener was patented in the 1850s. The manufacturing of tin cans by hand was a slow process; in the 1870s a tinsmith could make at best up to 50 tins per day.[38] As the process became more mechanised, production rates increased dramatically. By the early 20th century, Crosse and Blackwell's tin shop ledger of 1912–20 extends to over 200 pages and lists, by product per 100 tins, the stages of labour and the costs involved in each.[39] This sizeable document catalogues the full range of soups Crosse and Blackwell made and sold in tins (in ¼, ½, 1 pint (0.142, 0.284, 0.568 litres) and quart (1.137 litre) sizes;[40] and gallon (4.546 litre) size[41]), in addition to its small, medium and large curry tins[42] and the canned cheeses, including Parmesan, it made.[43] Tinned meat and fish feature heavily among its lines, with the meats including rolled tongue[44] and smoked ox tongue tins,[45] pressed beef in 1lb (0.454kg) tins,[46] ½lb and 1lb (0.227kg, 0.454kg) German sausage tins[47] (complementing their ½lb and 1lb Oxford[48] and same weight Cambridge sausages[49]), 1lb bacon,[50] large breakfast bacon[51] and 2lb (0.907kg) 'Wilts' back bacon tins[52] – ranges representing just a small proportion of the company's total tinned food output. The tin shop ledger of 1912–20 lists tin vacuum tops being made for Crosse and Blackwell's tinned rhubarb,[53] with the vacuum covers clearly being made in the tin shop.[54]

Whilst canned fruits, meat and fish appear to have been introduced by the likes of Sainsbury's in the 1890s,[55] food in tins for the domestic market remained mistrusted until at least the First World War (1914–18). There was a series of lead poisoning and food scandals during the last decade of the 19th and the first decade of the 20th century attributed to canning in tins, for example in Ireland where an individual was poisoned from cans of Crosse and Blackwell's oxtail soup,[56] but in particular in the United States.[57] Consumer concerns surrounding tin were summed up in a particularly alarmist article in 1910.[58] The importance, however, of tins as the container of choice for Crosse and Blackwell's 'Preserved Provisions For Use in the Navy and Army, for Yachts, Ship's Stores and Export to all Parts of the World' is nevertheless emphasised in its 'Wholesale Price list for January 1910' (not illustrated),[59] where a distinct range of product lines listed under this heading – bacon and lard, beef, Danish butter, cheese, cod and cod roes, cutlets, haddocks, halibut, hams, herring, mutton, poultry, sprats, sausages, tongues, turbot, veal, vegetables and whitebait – are all contained only in tins.

Glass

Glass containers were sourced from a series of different suppliers further afield, a situation remedied in 1920 after Crosse and Blackwell took a controlling interest in the glass jar and patent lid manufacturer, Alexander Cairns and Sons. Prior to this, although glass canning jars are present on the site, glass as a whole appears to have been mainly used for bottled table sauces and pickles rather than preserves[60] – a pattern reflected in the glass found on this site (below, 'Ceramics'; below, 4.2). During the Victorian period glass production was vastly increased by the invention of bottle-making machinery, made by Ashley at Ferrybridge (Yorkshire West Riding).[61] Further technological advances, first the development of semi-automatic bottle-making machines after 1882 and then the revolutionary introduction of the first fully automatic bottle-making machine in 1905 – developed in America by Michael Owens (the Owens Automatic Bottle Machine) – ushered glassmaking into being an industrialised process.[62] Later in the 1920s, making sheet glass made it possible to mass-produce jam jars in glass,[63] a technological innovation which led Hartley's to close its Caledonian pottery in Glasgow in 1928, 30 years after it had bought it to make and supply stoneware jam jars.[64]

By 1910, the wholesale price list for Crosse and Blackwell demonstrates how the company now sold a large proportion of its products in glass.[65] Sometimes shapes are referred to: castor bottles were filled with cayenne pepper,[66] and round and octagon bottles with glass stoppers were reserved for Captain White's Oriental Pickle.[67] The type of glass was often determined by measure or capacity (eg the ¼ to ½ pint (0.142–0.284 litre) glasses were used for 'Chicken Broth', 'Chicken Jelly'[68] and soups;[69] eg <129>, Fig 32) and the weight of the products they were filled with ('Lemon Cheese' was sold in ½lb (0.227kg) glasses[70]). References to the various methods of stoppering and sealing the company used are noted in the vacuum bottles ('Bottled Tart Fruits' and 'Fruits in syrup'[71]) and square bottles with lever stoppers (for 'Chutneys'[72]).

<129>

Fig 32 Colourless glass conical soup bottle <129> (scale *c* 1:2)

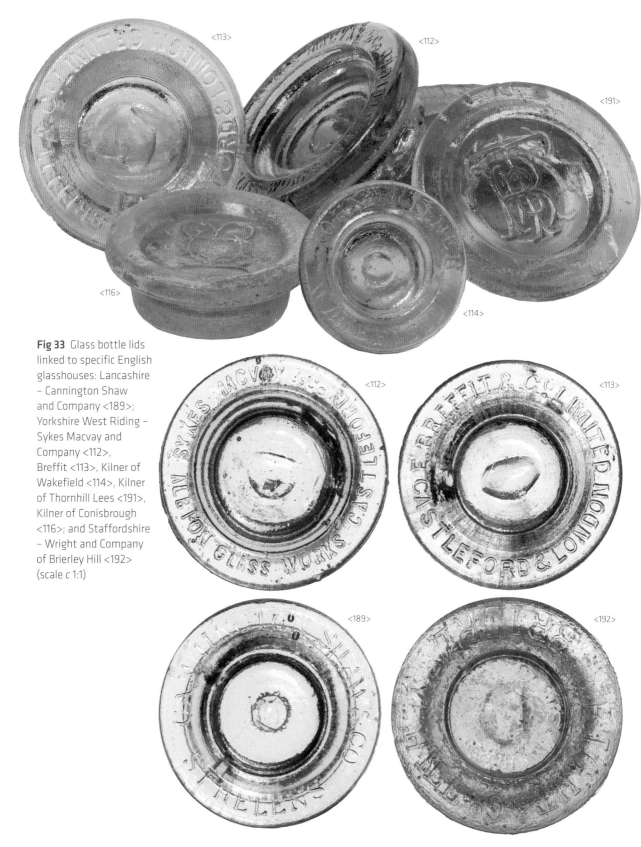

Fig 33 Glass bottle lids linked to specific English glasshouses: Lancashire – Cannington Shaw and Company <189>; Yorkshire West Riding – Sykes Macvay and Company <112>, Breffit <113>, Kilner of Wakefield <114>, Kilner of Thornhill Lees <191>, Kilner of Conisbrough <116>; and Staffordshire – Wright and Company of Brierley Hill <192> (scale *c* 1:1)

A large quantity of glass was recovered from the site, totalling 5741 fragments (123.096kg); stoppers are the main form, followed by bottles and jars (Table 1). When technologies can be determined most vessels are made in either semi-automatic or Owens automatic bottle-making machines. Most of the glass is unmarked and cannot be attributed to specific factories, but some lids (Fig 33) and bases have names or initials, and/or numbers and symbols that either refer to the maker, or to the bottle type patented and commissioned by the user, which shed some light on their suppliers. These demonstrate that Crosse and Blackwell sourced its glass from a selection of the major English glass manufacturers of the period, notably Cannington Shaw and Company of St Helens, Lancashire, and the various Yorkshire West Riding glassworks, in particular those based in Castleford. A number of lids with moulded lettering and symbols found on site show they were made by Cannington Shaw (<111>; <189>, Fig 33), Sykes Macvay and Company of the Albion glassworks (<112>, Fig 33), E Breffit and Company of the Aire and Calder Bottle Company (<113>, Fig 33), Kilner of Wakefield (1847–73) (<114>, Fig 33; <190>) and later at Thornhill Lees (1857–1920) (<115>; <191>, Fig 33) and Conisbrough (1863–1937) (<116>, Fig 33), and Rylands in Barnsley. Staffordshire glassmaking is represented by the lid made by Wright and Company of Brierley Hill (<192>, Fig 33).

Table 1 Quantification of the glass form assemblages by number of fragments, estimated number of vessels (ENV) and weight (kg)

Form	No. of fragments	ENV	Weight (kg)
Bottle	587	410	14373
Bottle/jar	333	236	6787
Ink bottle	1	1	103
Jar	283	179	12723
Phial	76	55	1118
Stopper	4410	4409	85030

Ceramics

The evidence from the site, in particular the filling of the cistern (S7; Chapter 2.1; Fig 16; Fig 17), demonstrated that ceramics – specifically durable stoneware and refined white earthenware – remained the container of choice for a range of Crosse and Blackwell products, such as the various mustards, vinegars, pickles, potted meats, meat extract, jams and marmalade it made. As noted, most of the pots were found discarded intact into the cistern (S7) with no evidence of the vessels being filled (New Building South: Chapter 2.1). This material, therefore, had either already been washed and processed through the returns department of the company, which dealt with 'thousands of empty ceramic and glass bottles and jars returned every day'[73] or had been stockpiled empty. Whilst the 12,000 or so pots discarded in the cistern must represent the largest quantity of pottery archaeologically retrieved in a single feature from London, an insight into the amount of stock kept by Britain's food manufacturers during the same period is provided by Hartley's Aintree warehouses, which were built to contain up to 15 million jars each.[74]

One of the pottery wares used by Crosse and Blackwell was stoneware. Its non-porous and high-temperature firing meant it was the ideal and preferred container (together with glass) for storing the more acidic pickles, vinegars and mustards made, with the corrosive environment created not suitable for earthenware. The various manufacturer stamps present on the English stoneware pots demonstrate that Crosse and Blackwell most often bought these durable hard-wearing containers from either C I C Bailey's west London Fulham pothouse (Bailey owned these premises in 1865–90[75]), James Stiff and Son's London pottery of Lambeth, south London, William Powell's Temple Gate pothouse in Bristol (Gloucestershire)[76] and Joseph Bourne and Sons of Denby (Derbyshire).[77] Feldspathic stoneware or English stoneware with Bristol glaze (ENGS BRST) (<P1> and <P2>, Fig 34) is the most common ware, with the products of Bourne's Derbyshire pothouse restricted to the English brown salt-glazed stoneware (ENGS) (<P3>, Fig 34) which include some vessels stamped 'C&B' close to the base (<P15>, Fig 36). The impressed 'C&B' proprietary stamp is applied to many other stoneware pots, and in addition to the Joseph Bourne made vessels; the products of Powell's Bristol pothouse found here also carry this stamp. All the pots are glazed inside. Details of all the illustrated pottery are in Table 2.

Green noted that Crosse and Blackwell's custom provided the mainstay of the Fulham pothouse's order book during the later 19th century following its acquisition of the London Vauxhall (in Lambeth) pottery's customers.[78] The radical mechanisation of stoneware production at the Fulham pottery after 1865 led to the increased production of preserving jars and bread crocks to meet the increasing demand for food containers.[79] The trade terminology for these stonewares detailed in two surviving 1873 published price lists of the products of Doulton and Watts[80] and James Stiff and Sons,[81] both of Lambeth, are of value for establishing contemporary terminology for the specific uses, capacities and prices for much of the stoneware used by Crosse and Blackwell at their London premises.

The archaeological evidence revealed that the company most often purchased different-sized 'bung jars' (<P1>–<P3>, Fig 34: found in five sizes[82]) in ½ pint to 3 quart (0.284–3.411 litres) measures and 1–6 gallon (c 4.546–27.276 litres) measures. Second are the 'upright bottles' (<P4>–<P6>, Fig 34) sold in ¼ to 3 quart (0.142–3.411 litres) and 1–6 gallon measures (in four sizes[83]). They also used an English stoneware with Bristol glaze (ENGS BRST) 'mustard jar' (<P7>, Fig 34[84]), supplied exclusively by Powell's Bristol Templegate pottery, and the 'wide-mouthed extract jar' (<P8>, Fig 34[85]), again found in a number of different sizes and displaying either a beaded or rouletted applied decoration. Less common are the four 'food jar' vessels (<P44>–<P46>, Fig 57[86]) found in Doulton's illustrated list as 'Registered air-tight covered jars for pickling and preserving' and fitted with the hermetically sealed lids with metal closures found on site (below, 4.3).

Providing insights into the intended contents are five paper labels for different products still affixed to the ENGS BRST and ENGS bung jars, which have

Cat no.	Context	Acc no.	Fabric	Form	Fig no.
<P1>	[149]	<143>	ENGS BRST	bung jar	34
<P2>	[149]	<144>	ENGS BRST	bung jar	34
<P3>	[149]	<145>	ENGS	bung jar	34
<P4>	[149]	<146>	ENGS BRST	upright bottle	34
<P5>	[149]	<147>	ENGS BRST	upright bottle	34
<P6>	[149]	<148>	ENGS BRST	upright bottle	34
<P7>	[43]	<149>	ENGS BRST	mustard jar	34
<P8>	[149]	<150>	ENGS BRST	wide-mouthed extract pot	34
<P9>	[149]	<151>	ENGS BRST	bung jar with label	35
<P10>	[149]	<152>	ENGS BRST	bung jar with label	35
<P11>	[19]	<153>	ENGS BRST	bung jar with label	35
<P12>	[149]	<154>	DERBS	bung jar with label	35
<P13>	[34]	<155>	ENGS BRST	bung jar with label	35
<P14>	[149]	<156>	ENGS BRST	bung jar with stamp	36
<P15>	[19]	<157>	ENGS BRST	bung jar with stamp	36
<P16>	[43]	<158>	ENGS BRST	mustard jar with batch no.	37
<P17>	[149]	<159>	ENGS BRST	bung jar with batch no.	37
<P18>	[149]	<160>	ENGS BRST	plain cylindrical jar	41
<P19>	[149]	<161>	ENGS BRST	plain cylindrical jar	41
<P20>	[149]	<162>	ENGS BRST	plain cylindrical jar	41
<P21>	[149]	<163>	ENGS BRST	plain cylindrical jar	41
<P22>	[149]	<164>	ENGS BRST	plain cylindrical jar	41
<P23>	[149]	<165>	REFW	plain cylindrical jar	41
<P24>	[43]	<166>	REFW	grooved cylindrical jar	41
<P25>	[14]	<167>	REFW	grooved cylindrical jar	44
<P26>	[14]	<168>	REFW	grooved cylindrical jar	44
<P27>	[14]	<169>	REFW	grooved cylindrical jar	44
<P28>	[14]	<170>	REFW	grooved cylindrical jar	44
<P29>	[14]	<171>	REFW	grooved cylindrical jar	44
<P30>	[14]	<172>	REFW	grooved cylindrical jar	44
<P31>	[14]	<173>	REFW	grooved cylindrical jar	44
<P32>	[19]	<174>	REFW	plain cylindrical jar	44
<P33>	[149]	<175>	REFW	plain shouldered jar	44
<P34>	[149]	<176>	REFW	plain shouldered jar with label	45
<P35>	[34]	<177>	REFW	grooved cylindrical jar with label	45
<P36>	[149]	<178>	REFW	plain cylindrical jar with label	45
<P37>	[149]	<179>	REFW	grooved cylindrical jar with label	45
<P38>	[34]	<180>	REFW	plain cylindrical jar with label	45
<P39>	[34]	<181>	REFW	plain cylindrical jar with label	45
<P40>	[43]	<187>	TPW2	ginger jar	46
<P41>	[43]	<188>	TPW2	ginger jar	46
<P42>	[43]	<182>	ENGS BRST	mustard jar	57
<P43>	[43]	<183>	ENGS BRST	mustard jar	57
<P44>	[149]	<184>	ENGS BRST	food jar	57
<P45>	[149]	<185>	ENGS BRST	food jar	57
<P46>	[149]	<186>	ENGS BRST	food jar	57

Table 2 Details of illustrated pottery <P1>–<P46>

survived from excavation. The first label is for Crosse and Blackwell's Piccalilli (<P9>, Fig 35). Their preserve range is represented by the Pure Orange Marmalade (<P10>, Fig 35) and Household Jam (<P11>, Fig 35) labels and the fourth, for another unspecified jam product (<P12>, Fig 35), representing the only label still applied to the brown-glazed Derbyshire stoneware (DERBS) bung jars. Another partially surviving label applied to a bung jar (<P13>, Fig 35) advertises 'GROUND SWEET…', and can be matched to the ground sweet almonds Crosse and Blackwell sold.[87]

Another method of proof of ownership was via the application of impressed stamped lettering to a pot by the manufacturer. Crosse and Blackwell, therefore, followed the custom and practice of a number of retailers[88] by having stoneware pots made that additionally carried the lettering 'CROSSE & BLACKWELL/OILMEN/21 SOHO SQUARE' applied to the upper half of a number of jars (<P14>, Fig 36).

Exclusive to the stoneware are the various bung jars in English stoneware with Bristol glaze (ENGS BRST) and English brown salt-glazed stoneware (ENGS) and ENGS BRST mustard jars which have numbers crudely painted in blue and black by Crosse and Blackwell on the underside of some bases.

Fig 34 A selection of English stoneware vessels: bung jars <P1> and <P2>, with Bristol glaze, and brown salt-glazed <P3>; upright bottles <P4>, <P5> and <P6> (max height 260mm) with Bristol glaze; mustard jar <P7> with Bristol glaze; and wide-mouthed extract jar <P8> with Bristol glaze (scale c 1:4)

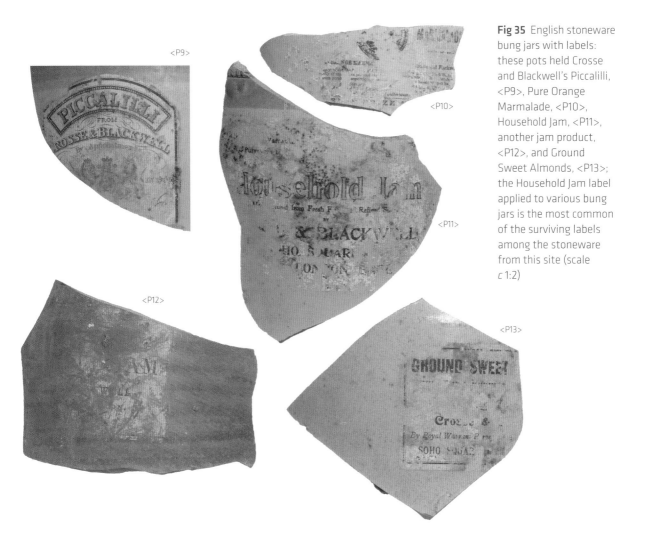

<P9>

<P10>

<P11>

<P12>

<P13>

Fig 35 English stoneware bung jars with labels: these pots held Crosse and Blackwell's Piccalilli, <P9>, Pure Orange Marmalade, <P10>, Household Jam, <P11>, another jam product, <P12>, and Ground Sweet Almonds, <P13>; the Household Jam label applied to various bung jars is the most common of the surviving labels among the stoneware from this site (scale *c* 1:2)

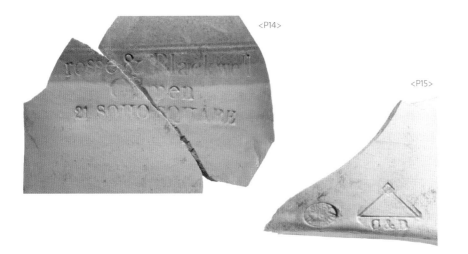

<P14>

<P15>

Fig 36 Examples of English stoneware with Bristol glaze bung jars with stamps: <P14> stamped 'CROSSE & BLACKWELL/OILMEN/ 21 SOHO SQUARE'; and <P15> stamped (right) 'C&B' with a triangular symbol and (left) 'SKEY/13/TAMWORTH' (scale *c* 1:2)

<P16>

Mustard jars are marked with the number '15' in blue paint only (<P16>, Fig 37); black painted two or three numbers are used on bung jars separated by a full stop after the first digit, with the numbers 1, 3.1, 3.2, 3.4, 3.6, 3.8, 4.5, 6.2, 6.10 best represented. Only one continuous sequence between 3.11 and 3.15 is evident (eg <P17>, Fig 37). The reason for their application is unknown, but it is suggested here that they reflect a stocktaking method or are related to their place of storage on shelves within Crosse and Blackwell's premises.

Fig 37 Examples of English stoneware vessels with Bristol glaze and batch numbers painted on the base: mustard pot <P16> with '15'; and bung jar <P17> with '3.13' (scale *c* 1:2)

<P17>

4.2 Crosse and Blackwell's products and packaging identified in the assemblage

Whilst the range of tin, glass and ceramic containers employed by Crosse and Blackwell found on the site have been introduced above, this section discusses the surviving evidence for the various products the company sold. For consistency, the titles and headings of the various identified product lines (below) follow those in Crosse and Blackwell's January 1910, wholesale price list,[89] with the date of this catalogue also closely corresponding to that of the latest glass and ceramic assemblages found on this site.

The attribution of the containers and vessels found to the specific products they once contained has been achieved through a series of sources. Firstly, the different labels that have survived affixed to the various pots and glass found on this site are invaluable. These have demonstrated, for example, how the stoneware bung jars contained the Crosse and Blackwell products Piccalilli, Household Jam, Pure Orange Marmalade and Ground Sweet Almonds. The labels applied to some of the thousands of 1lb (0.454kg) white ware cylindrical jars indicate that this assemblage was meant for its various flavoured jams, while the Pure Orange Marmalade labels affixed to both the refined white earthenware and stoneware vessels show how the same product could be stored in containers made of different materials. The labels also demonstrate that certain containers were intended/designed for specific products, for example the stoneware pots used for mustard, or the upright bottles that contained vinegars.

Secondly, the three Crosse and Blackwell price lists that have survived from the time when the company occupied Soho, from 1846 (Fig 38),[90] 1873 (Fig 39)[91] and 1910,[92] are also useful for determining the containers used and how these changed during the Victorian period up to the end of the Edwardian

Fig 38 Crosse and Blackwell's price list for 1846

(LMA, 4467/G/03/002, 105)

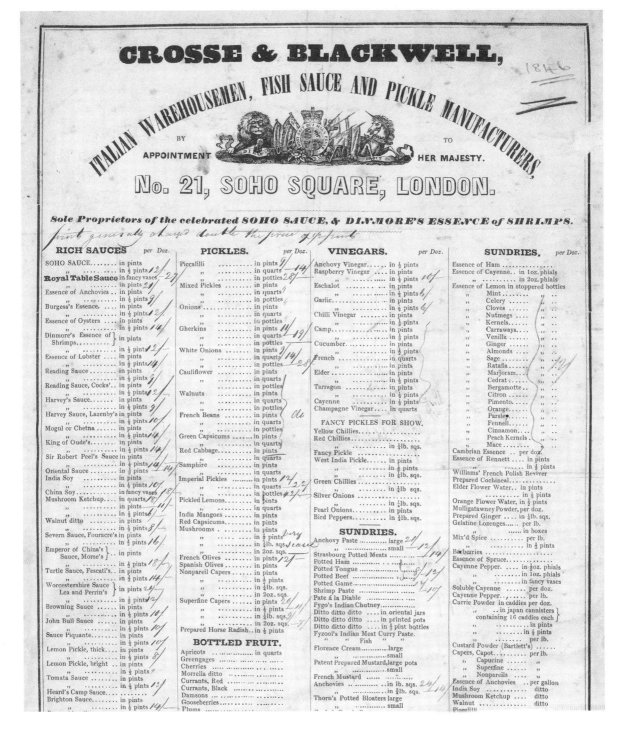

period. The first 1846 price list documents the firm's products under rich sauces, pickles, bottled fruit, preserves, vinegars and sundries headings. Measure size, by capacity (½ pints, pints, quarts) or weight (in oz or lb), is listed by each product, together with cost. When containers are noted, tin is reserved for just a few products (notably 'Salmon'), with packets (for 'Potatoe Flour', 'Arrow Root' to 'Tous les mois') and boxes (containing 'Gelatine Lozenges', 'Genoa Vermicelli' to 'Genoa Maccaroni') similarly infrequent. Glass appears to be used for the numerous essences sold (eg of lemon, mint and ginger to name just a few) in 'stoppered bottles', with 'phials' reserved for essence of cayenne and cayenne pepper.

By 1873, the monthly price list for October of that year (Fig 39) is more specific in cataloguing how the same product could be packaged in many different materials.[93] For example, pickles were filled in jars or casks, mustard

Fig 39 Crosse and Blackwell's monthly price list for October 1873
(LMA, 4467/G/03/002, 187–8)

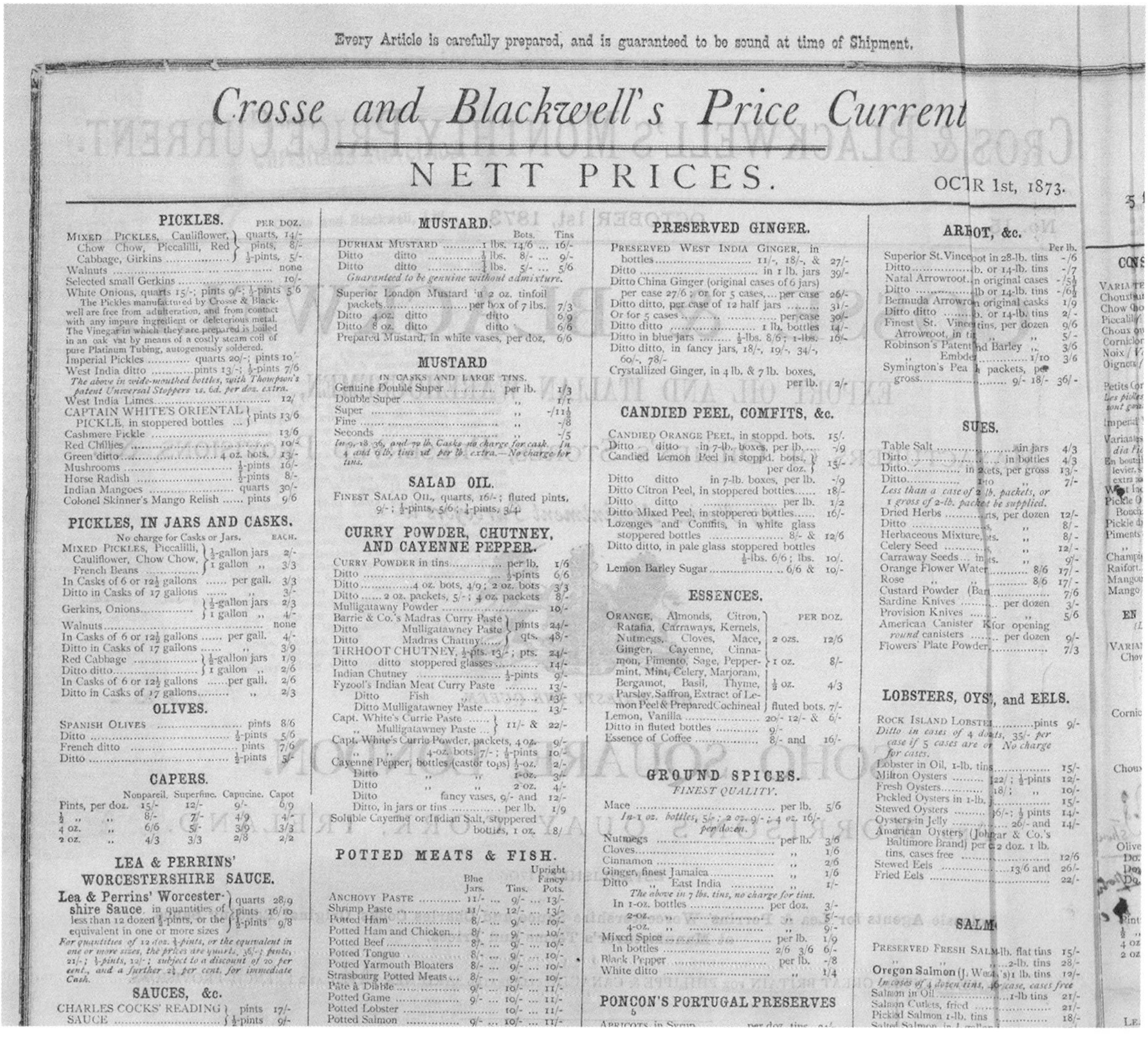
Every Article is carefully prepared, and is guaranteed to be sound at time of Shipment.

Crosse and Blackwell's Price Current

NETT PRICES.

OCTR 1st, 1873.

PICKLES. PER DOZ.
MIXED PICKLES, Cauliflower, Chow Chow, Piccalilli, Red Cabbage, Girkins ... quarts, 14/- ; pints, 8/- ; ½-pints, 5/-
Walnuts ... none
Selected small Gerkins ... 10/-
White Onions, quarts 15/-; pints 9/-; ½-pints 5/6
The Pickles manufactured by Crosse & Blackwell are free from adulteration, and from contact with any impure ingredient or deleterious metal. The Vinegar in which they are prepared is boiled in an oak vat by means of a costly steam coil of pure Platinum Tubing, autogenously soldered.
Imperial Pickles ... quarts 20/-; pints 10/-
West India ditto ... pints 13/-; ½-pints 7/6
The above in wide-mouthed bottles, with Thompson's patent Universal Stoppers 1s. 6d. per doz. extra.
West India Limes ... 12/
CAPTAIN WHITE'S ORIENTAL PICKLE, in stoppered bottles ... pints 13/6
Cashmere Pickle ... 13/6
Red Chillies ... 10/-
Green ditto ... 4 oz. bots. 13/-
Mushrooms ... ½-pints 16/-
Horse Radish ... ½-pints 8/-
Indian Mangoes ... quarts 30/-
Colonel Skinner's Mango Relish ... pints 9/6

PICKLES, IN JARS AND CASKS.
No charge for Casks or Jars. EACH.
MIXED PICKLES, Piccalilli, Cauliflower, Chow Chow, French Beans ... ½-gallon jars 2/- ; 1 gallon ,, 3/3
In Casks of 6 or 12½ gallons ... per gall. 3/3
Ditto in Casks of 17 gallons ... ,, 3/-
Gerkins, Onions ... ½-gallon jars 2/3 ; 1 gallon ,, 4/-
Walnuts ... none
In Casks of 6 or 12½ gallons ... per gall. 4/-
Ditto in Casks of 17 gallons ... ,, 3/9
Red Cabbage ... ½-gallon jars 1/9
Ditto ditto ... 1 gallon ,, 2/6
In Casks of 6 or 12½ gallons ... per gall. 2/6
Ditto in Casks of 17 gallons ... ,, 2/3

OLIVES.
SPANISH OLIVES ... pints 8/6
Ditto ... ½-pints 5/6
French ditto ... pints 7/6
Ditto ... ½-pints 5/-

CAPERS.

	Nonpareil.	Superfine.	Capucine.	Capot
Pints, per doz.	15/-	12/-	9/-	6/9
½ ,, ,,	8/-	7/-	4/9	4/-
4 oz. ,,	6/6	5/-	3/9	3/3
2 oz. ,,	4/3	3/3	2/8	2/2

LEA & PERRINS' WORCESTERSHIRE SAUCE.
Lea & Perrins' Worcestershire Sauce, in quantities of less than 12 dozen ½-pints, or the equivalent in one or more sizes ... quarts 28/9 ; pints 16/10 ; ½-pints 9/8
For quantities of 12 doz. ½-pints, or the equivalent in one or more sizes, the prices are quarts, 36/-; pints, 21/-; ½-pints, 12/-; subject to a discount of 20 per cent., and a further 2½ per cent. for immediate Cash.

SAUCES, &c.
CHARLES COCKS' READING SAUCE ... pints 17/- ; ½-pints 9/-

MUSTARD.

		Bots.	Tins
DURHAM MUSTARD	1 lbs.	14/6	16/-
Ditto ditto	½ lbs.	8/-	9/-
Ditto ditto	¼ lbs.	5/-	5/6

Guaranteed to be genuine without admixture.
Superior London Mustard in 2 oz. tinfoil packets ... per box of 7 lbs. 7/3
Ditto 4 oz. ditto ditto 6/9
Ditto 8 oz. ditto ditto 6/6
Prepared Mustard, in white vases, per doz, 6/6

MUSTARD
IN CASKS AND LARGE TINS.
Genuine Double Super ... per lb. 1/3
Double Super ... ,, 1/1
Super ... ,, -/11½
Fine ... ,, -/8
Seconds ... ,, -/5
In 9, 18, 36, and 72 lb. Casks no charge for cask. In 4 and 6 lb. tins 1d. per lb. extra.—No charge for tins.

SALAD OIL.
FINEST SALAD OIL, quarts, 16/-; fluted pints, 9/-; ½-pints, 5/6; ¼-pints, 3/4.

CURRY POWDER, CHUTNEY, AND CAYENNE PEPPER.
CURRY POWDER in tins ... per lb. 1/6
Ditto ... ½-pints 6/6
Ditto ... 4 oz. bots, 4/9; 2 oz. bots 3/3
Ditto ... 2 oz. packets, 5/-; 4 oz. packets 8/-
Mulligatawny Powder ... 10/-
Barrie & Co.'s Madras Curry Paste / Ditto Mulligatawney Paste / Ditto Madras Chattny ... pints 24/- ; qts. 48/-
TIRHOOT CHUTNEY, ½-pts. 13/-; pts. 24/-
Ditto ditto stoppered glasses ... 14/-
Indian Chutney ... ½-pints 9/-
Fyzool's Indian Meat Curry Paste ... 13/-
Ditto Fish ,, ... 13/-
Ditto Mulligatawney Paste ... 13/-
Capt. White's Currie Paste / ,, Mulligatawney Paste ... 11/- & 22/-
Capt. White's Currie Powder, packets, 4 oz. 9/-
,, ,, 4-oz. bots. 7/-; ½-pints 10/-
Cayenne Pepper, bottles (castor tops) ½-oz. 2/-
Ditto ,, ,, 1-oz. 3/-
Ditto ,, ,, 2 oz. 4/-
Ditto fancy vases, 9/- and 12/-
Ditto, in jars or tins ... per lb. 1/9
Soluble Cayenne or Indian Salt, stoppered bottles, 1 oz. 8/

POTTED MEATS & FISH.

	Blue Jars.	Tins.	Upright Fancy Pots.
ANCHOVY PASTE	11/-	9/-	13/-
Shrimp Paste	11/-	12/-	13/-
Potted Ham	8/-	9/-	10/-
Potted Ham and Chicken	8/-	9/-	10/-
Potted Beef	8/-	9/-	10/-
Potted Tongue	8/-	9/-	10/-
Potted Yarmouth Bloaters	8/-	9/-	10/-
Strasbourg Potted Meats	8/-	9/-	10/-
Pâte à Diable	9/-	10/-	11/-
Potted Game	9/-	10/-	11/-
Potted Lobster		10/-	11/-
Potted Salmon	9/-	10/-	11/-

PRESERVED GINGER.
PRESERVED WEST INDIA GINGER, in bottles ... 11/-, 18/-, & 27/-
Ditto ... in 1 lb. jars 39/-
Ditto China Ginger (original cases of 6 jars) per case 27/6; or for 5 cases, ... per case 26/-
Ditto ditto, per case of 12 half jars ... 31/-
Or for 5 cases ... per case 30/-
Ditto ditto ... 1 lb. bottles 14/-
Ditto in blue jars ... ½-lbs. 8/6; 1-lbs. 16/-
Ditto ditto, in fancy jars, 18/-, 19/-, 34/-, 60/-, 78/-
Crystallized Ginger, in 4 lb. & 7 lb. boxes, per lb. 2/-

CANDIED PEEL, COMFITS, &c.
CANDIED ORANGE PEEL, in stoppd. bots. 15/.
Ditto ditto in 7-lb. boxes, per lb. -/9
Candied Lemon Peel in stoppd. bots. per doz. 15/-
Ditto ditto in 7-lb. boxes, per lb. -/9
Ditto Citron Peel, in stoppered bottles ... 18/-
Ditto ditto ... per lb. 1/2
Ditto Mixed Peel, in stoppered bottles ... 16/-
Lozenges and Comfits, in white glass stoppered bottles ... 8/- & 12/6
Ditto ditto, in pale glass stoppered bottles ½-lbs. 6/6; lbs. 10/.
Lemon Barley Sugar ... 6/6 & 10/-

ESSENCES.
ORANGE, Almonds, Citron, Ratafia, Carraways, Kernels, Nutmegs, Cloves, Mace, Ginger, Cayenne, Cinnamon, Pimento, Sage, Peppermint, Mint, Celery, Marjoram, Bergamot, Basil, Thyme, Parsley, Saffron, Extract of Lemon Peel & Prepared Cochineal ... PER DOZ. 2 ozs. 12/6 ; 1 oz. 8/- ; ½ oz. 4/3 ; fluted bots. 7/-
Lemon, Vanilla ... 20/- 12/- & 6/-
Ditto in fluted bottles ... 9/-
Essence of Coffee ... 8/- and 16/-

GROUND SPICES.
FINEST QUALITY.
Mace ... per lb. 5/6
In 1 oz. bottles, 5/-; 2 oz. 9/-; 4 oz. 16/- per dozen.
Nutmegs ... per lb. 3/6
Cloves ... ,, 1/6
Cinnamon ... ,, 2/6
Ginger, finest Jamaica ... ,, 1/6
Ditto ,, East India ... ,, 1/-
The above in 7 lbs. tins, no charge for tins.
In 1-oz. bottles ... per doz. 3/-
2-oz. ,, ... ,, 5/-
4-oz. ,, ... ,, 9/-
Mixed Spice ... per lb. 1/9
In bottles ... 2/6 3/6 6/-
Black Pepper ... per lb. -/8
White ditto ... ,, 1/4

PONCON'S PORTUGAL PRESERVES

ARROWROOT, &c.
Per lb.
Superior St. Vince[...]oot in 28-lb. tins -/6
Ditto ... [...]b. or 14-lb. tins -/7
Natal Arrowroot [...]n original cases -/5½
Ditto ... [...]lb or 14-lb. tins -/6½
Bermuda Arrowro[...]n original casks 1/9
Ditto ditto ... [...]b. or 14-lb. tins 2/-
Finest St. Vince[...] Arrowroot, in ti[...] tins, per dozen 9/6 ; ,, ,, 5/-
Robinson's Patent [...]nd Barley ,, 3/6
,, Embde[...] ... 1/10 3/6
Symington's Pea [...] packets, per gross ... 9/- 18/- 36/-

S[...]ES.
Table Salt ... in jars 4/3
Ditto ... in bottles 4/3
Ditto ... in [...]kets, per gross 13/-
Ditto ... ,, 7/-
Less than a case of [...] lb. packets, or 1 gross of 2-lb. packe[...] be supplied.
Dried Herbs ... [...]ts, per dozen 12/-
Ditto ... ,, 8/-
Herbaceous Mixture, [...] ,, 8/-
Celery Seed ... ,, 12/-
Carraway Seeds ... in [...] ,, 9/-
Orange Flower Water ... 8/6 17/-
Rose ,, ,, ... 8/6 17/-
Custard Powder (Bar[...] ... 7/6
Sardine Knives ... per dozen 3/-
Provision Knives ... ,, 5/6
American Canister K[...] for opening *round* canisters ... per dozen 9/-
Flowers' Plate Powder ... 7/3

LOBSTERS, OYS[...], and EELS.
ROCK ISLAND LOBSTE[...] ... pints 9/-
Ditto in cases of 4 do[...], 35/- per case if 5 cases are o[...] No charge for cases.
Lobster in Oil, 1-lb. tins ... 15/-
Milton Oysters ... [...]22/; ½-pints 12/-
Fresh Oysters ... [...]18/; ,, 10/-
Pickled Oysters in 1-lb. [...] ... 15/-
Stewed Oysters ... [...]6/-; ½ pints 14/-
Oysters in Jelly ... 26/- and 14/-
American Oysters (Jo[...]ar & Co.'s Baltimore Brand) per [...] 2 doz. 1 lb. tins, cases free ... 12/6
Stewed Eels ... 13/6 and 26/-
Fried Eels ... 22/-

SALM[...]
PRESERVED FRESH SAL[...]-lb. flat tins 15/-
,, ,, ... 2-lb. tins 28/-
Oregon Salmon (J. We[...]'s) 1 lb. tins 19/-
In cases of 4 dozen tins, [...] case, cases free
Salmon in Oil ... 1-lb tins 21/-
Salmon Cutlets, fried ... 21/-
Pickled Salmon 1-lb. tins ... 18/-

in bottles, tins or casks; curry powder, chutney and cayenne pepper could be found in bottles, stoppered bottles and packets, with potted meats and fish in blue jars, tins and upright fancy pots. Crosse and Blackwell's popular jams, jellies and marmalades filled plain pots or glass; preserved ginger was in bottles, half jars or blue jars, candied peels, comfits and such like in stoppered bottles, boxes or white glass, tapioca and sago in tins and bottles, arrowroot in tins and packets, herring in both tins and bottles and sundries in packets and bottles.

A number of products, however, remained wedded to a single container, with salad oils sold in fluted pints (presumably glass), prepared jellies and creams in glass jars, fruits in syrup in white glass bottles, essences in fluted bottles (again presumed here as glass), ground spices, salmon and Puncon's Portugal preserves solely packaged in tins, with Extractum Carnis in pots. Soups were marketed in packets. The containers used for some of their most important lines, notably olives, capers, Lea & Perrins Worcestershire Sauce, sauces, John Burgess and Son's preparations (anchovies), sole, haddock and so forth are not specified, and are instead listed by the weight or liquid measures they were sold in and by price. It can be presumed from the stoppers, however, that Lea & Perrins Worcestershire Sauce and other sauces were in glass bottles.

Thirdly, comparison of the wholesale price list for January 1910[94] with the first illustrated export price list of 1923[95] – which presents a full account of Crosse and Blackwell's 63 product lines arranged with their labels, how they were canned and details of their carriage and price – can also help to assess the change in the materials Crosse and Blackwell employed to package its products (Chapter 5; Chapter 6) and to link the various pot and glass containers found on the site to a particular product, notably Mushroom Catsup (ketchup)[96] and Florence Cream bottles.[97]

'Essences' (product no. 22)

The 1868 inventory[98] records how 21 Soho Square (Chapter 2.1; Fig 5) contained an essence room and the first vessels that have been attributed to a documented Crosse and Blackwell product are the two forms found on the site, both in colourless glass, probably used for a concentrated sauce or essence; 40 of the 55 examples were found in the fills of the cistern (S7; [19], [131] and [149]; Fig 13; Fig 16; Fig 17) with the others in the various underfloor levelling deposits ([34], [36], [43]) located in New Building South (Fig 5, building C). The first type, represented by 19 examples, is of squat cylindrical form (height *c* 78mm) with narrow cylindrical neck; two in the cistern fill [149] have the letter 'M' or 'W' on the underside, while another from the filling of this feature, [19], has the letters 'DD' on the base. Of the four complete examples of this type found, one has the remains of its original label (<130>, Fig 40). The second type (sizes vary slightly: heights 82mm, 85mm,

<130>

<131>

Fig 40 Small glass essence bottles: cylindrical with remains of the label, <130>; and with lentoid section, <131> (scale *c* 1:1)

88mm), represented by 36 examples, has a distinctive lentoid section and cylindrical neck, as typified by <131> (Fig 40). The 1910 wholesale price list[99] notes flavoured essences from almonds, cloves, ginger, nutmeg, sage and vanilla, to name a few,[100] and in the similar 1873 list essences are noted as sold in various ounce sizes in fluted glass bottles.[101]

'Extractum Carnis' (product no. 25)

This represents a popular concentrated meat extract product first credited to the German Justus Van Liebig[102] and sold during the Victorian and Edwardian periods. Crosse and Blackwell used small stoneware jars (eg <P18>–<P22>, Fig 41) in three sizes to can this product. These vessels were likely to have been cork-stoppered and then fitted with a tin foil or parchment cap – Sainsbury's bloater fish paste was sealed in pots in this fashion.[103] The (partial) labels that have survived on two of the English stoneware jars with Bristol glaze (ENGS BRST) show that they contained this particular meat extract.

'Potted Meats & Fish' (product no. 47)

The 1868 inventory records how the Sutton Street part of New Building South (Chapter 2.1; Fig 5, building C) sustained a range of meat processing and anchovy-making equipment, with 21 Soho Square (Fig 5, building A) also containing a meat room.[104] The wholesale price list for January 1910[105] lists potted beef, chicken, game, hams, turkey (sometimes with tongue) and Strasbourg meats among its potted meats, which were contained in tins with

Fig 41 Plain cylindrical English stoneware with Bristol glaze jars <P18>–<P22> (middle of three sizes found) used for Extractum Carnis and plain <P23> or grooved <P24> small cylindrical refined white earthenware jars used for potted meats (scale *c* 1:2)

    CROSSE AND BLACKWELL 1830–1921

keys, corked jars or vacuum glass.[106] The corresponding potted fish lines of lobster, salmon, crab and prawn paste were also sold in vacuum glass. For anchovy and bloater pastes, Crosse and Blackwell employed tins, corked jars, vacuum glass, patent pots and flat pots. From the site a number of small glass cylindrical jars and refined white earthenware pots, either plain (<P23>, Fig 41) or vertically grooved (<P24>, Fig 41), have been attributed to the 'Potted Meats & Fish' product range respectively.

Up to 15 glass containers have been attributed to potted meats: two small jars have a band of vertical ribbing below the rim, one squat (<132>, height 49mm), the other taller (<135>, Fig 42). Twelve examples in one of the cistern (S7) fills, [19] (Fig 16; Fig 17), are plain 'tumbler'-shaped jars of slightly differing sizes, all in colourless glass (eg <134>, Fig 42: known heights 81mm and 110mm); one example bears part of a worn paper label with the words 'LONDON ENGLAND' at the base. Some bases have Owens-type valve marks, showing they date to the early 20th century.

'Household Jam', 'Jams & Jellies' and 'Pure Orange Marmalade' (product nos 33, 34 and 42)

A significant component of both the glass and ceramic assemblages found on site is related to the Household Jam, Jams & Jellies, and Pure Orange Marmalade Crosse and Blackwell made. These three products are considered together here as they are similar foods and as such were all bottled in similar pots and glass jars. We have seen how jam making by Crosse and Blackwell was begun in 1840 (Chapter 2.1).[107] The production processes were carried out in one room in Little Denmark Street (Fig 28), which had to accommodate the fruit,[108] but as the factory expanded and premises became more cramped, strawberries were sometimes hulled outdoors, the waste being thrown into the gutter.[109] The finished product was stored at 21 Soho Square which contained the jam jar warehouse, with New Building South also containing a jam room.

The most distinctive type of glass jar found on the site is the large cylindrical shouldered form with a short neck and bead rim finish, made in natural green glass (c 60 examples, 107 sherds), with one complete example (<138>, Fig 43; height 173mm) found in one of the levelling deposits, [34], located in New Building South (Chapter 2.1; Fig 5, building C). These vessels are the glass equivalents of the bung jar shape made in stoneware; they were probably closed with a glass lid or cork bung, numerous examples of which were also found (below, 4.3). Whilst we cannot be certain what they contained, the illustrated export price list for 1923 shows this shape was used for jams[110] and jellies.[111] The 22 measurable bases fall into two main size groups (c 106–107mm diameter and a smaller 90–97mm diameter), identified among the 60 identifiable vessels (from 109 sherds). One large base from Castleford Bottle

<134>

<135>

Fig 42 Glass jars <134> and <135> for potted meat and meat pastes (scale *c* 1:2)

Company was found in the cistern fill. Most sherds with moulded lettering come from Cannington Shaw of St Helens (above, 4.1), but two sherds bear the letters 'C.S & Co' and nine have 'C.S & Co Ld' with one of these also having the initials 'C & B' (<137>). In addition, there are three bases made by Kilner, marked 'J K & S', 'KBC' and 'K', found in various underfloor make-up deposits in New Building South, the first of which also has the remains of an applied label on the body. A further 79 jars (up to 119 sherds) are probably of the same cylindrical form but lack the upper body; base diameters range between 77mm and 98mm with moulded lettering on up to eight examples showing they were made in the same glasshouses. Several bases have individual patent or manufacturers' numbers, with or without lettering. One reads '157', while the others include the numbers '2024', '3704' (two examples), '4038', '4093' and '?096'.

Also in natural green glass are two necked jars from [36], one of the levelling deposits associated with New Building South, both with a distinctive grooved and bevelled rim form that may have been designed to fit a metal cap.

Some 35 colourless cylindrical glass jars (46 sherds) were also found, one of which has a high angular shoulder, constricted neck and everted rim for tying a covering of paper or cloth. Like the 'tumbler' meat paste jars, these are clearly a later development, as some bases have valve or ejection marks on the underside that suggest they were made in semi-automatic and automatic non-Owens bottle machines; if this is the case, they must date to the first decade

Fig 43 Glass jar <138> made by Kilner (scale *c* 1:2)

<138>

of the 20th century, or later, when this technology was introduced. Some also have symbols on the underside, including numbers in a triangle and a blank six-pointed star, and one with the letters 'B & C Co', while a body sherd from [19], one of the cistern (S7) fills, has the remains of a label stating 'FRESH'. Finally, there are 18 sherds from three smaller or narrower cylindrical forms and three from two straight-sided jars. No rim forms were found that would be suited to a wax seal closure, nor do any have the external screw threads seen on American 'mason jars' or later Kilner jars.

By 1860 Crosse and Blackwell was making marmalade from Seville oranges in platinum or silver pans to ensure the highest quality (Chapter 6.1). In addition to glass jars, jams or marmalade were also packed in the larger horizontally grooved refined white earthenware (REFW) cylindrical jars (<P25>–<P31>, Fig 44), large numbers of which were found, especially in the cistern (S7; Chapter 2.1; Fig 16; Fig 17). Stamped on the underside of the base denoting their 'lb' size they additionally carry the stamp of 'Maling Newcastle' (<P31>, Fig 44), advertising them as the products of C T Maling's Ford A and B pottery in Newcastle, which had switched from making food containers by hand to machine in the 1850s.[112] The scale of the production this allowed is demonstrated in the records of just one of Maling's customers, the confectioners and preserve manufacturers Keiller and Sons of Dundee (Angus, Scotland) (Crosse and Blackwell acquired this company as a subsidiary in 1918). By the 1870s Keiller and Sons were ordering millions of the jars per year to fill with their preserves (notably marmalade[113]). A second group common to the site are the plain cylindrical jars (<P32>, Fig 44) in various sizes and a third, in a shape similar to the stoneware bung jars (above, 4.1; Fig 34), are the plain shouldered jars (<P33>, Fig 44). Of one size, these last heavier-bodied REFW jars are also stamped 'Maling Newcastle' or 'Maling Newcastle Two

Fig 44 Grooved cylindrical refined white earthenware jars <P25>-<P31> (max height 95mm), made by the Newcastle factory Maling, and plain cylindrical <P32> and plain shouldered <P33> refined white earthenware jars (scale *c* 1:4)

Pounds' on their base. The most frequent label design found demonstrates that they once contained Crosse and Blackwell's Pure Orange Marmalade, a label which proudly boasts this product was made from Seville oranges (<P34>, Fig 45). The various black-coloured paper labels that have survived from the site, from both the grooved and plain cylindrical jars, show that the majority once held raspberry (<P35> and <P36>, Fig 45), redcurrant (<P37>, Fig 45) and plum jams (<P38>, Fig 45) or orange marmalade (<P39>, Fig 45).

Fig 45 Plain shouldered refined white earthenware jar <P34> with Pure Orange Marmalade label, and selection of labelled refined white earthenware examples for raspberry, <P35> and <P36>, redcurrant, <P37>, and plum jam, <P38>, and orange marmalade, <P39> (scale *c* 1:2)

'Preserved Ginger' (product no. 46)

Found only in [43], one of the various underfloor make-up deposits located in New Building South (Chapter 2.1; Fig 5, building C), were up to 44 refined white ware jars with underglaze blue transfer-printed decoration (TPW2) (<P40> and <P41>, Fig 46). These ¼lb or ½lb (0.113kg or 0.227kg) measure containers held Crosse and Blackwell's Preserved Ginger product, a product shown in these jars in the illustrated export price list for 1923[114] (the third 1lb (0.454kg) size available was, however, sold just in tins). Ginger was imported from West Africa, the Caribbean (Jamaica) or Asia (India) and the Far East (eg Japan, China), and was the principal ingredient for various Victorian cake and pudding recipes. Whilst these jars are presumed as British made not stamped with a manufacturer's name, they are decorated with a chinoiserie printed design, reflecting both the exotic contents and the continuing popularity and familiarity of the willow pattern print.[115] The noted illustrated export price list presents these jars sealed with a similarly decorated ceramic lid tied by a ribbon.

<P40>

<P41>

Fig 46 Refined white ware ginger jars <P40> and <P41> with underglaze blue transfer-printed decoration (scale *c* 1:2)

'Pickles' and 'Pickles in Jars' (product nos 48 and 49)

By 1910 Crosse and Blackwell marketed an extensive range of pickles in jars (notably Piccalilli, below), with its cauliflower, chow chow, gherkins, piccalilli, red cabbage, walnuts and various onions sold in corked bottles[116] and its Captain White's Oriental Pickle contained in round or octagonal bottles with either lever or glass stoppers. The making of pickles appears to have been established by Crosse and Blackwell's predecessors West and Wyatt,[117] and pickle remained an integral part of Crosse and Blackwell's product line for both its home and export market (Chapter 5.2). To better facilitate this range, a separate export pickle factory was set up in Stacey Street in 1878 (Chapter 2.1; Fig 6) but moved in 1884 to the large and purpose-built premises of Soho Wharf near Westminster Bridge (Chapter 5.2). The importance of the export market, considered later (Chapter 5.2), can be seen in the names it applied to

Fig 47 Illustration of the old pickle filling department in a 1920 edition of the *Square Magazine*: this is likely to have been located in either the New Building South factory or in 20 Soho Square (LMA, 4467/G/03/003, February–April 1920, 13)

<128>

Fig 48 Colourless glass pickle bottle <128>, biconical with Greek key pattern (scale *c* 1:2)

its pickle range, with Imperial Pickles, West India Pickles, India Mangoes, Col Skinner's Mango Relish and West India Limes reflecting Britain's global reach. Branston Pickle was a later development, named after the new factory site near Burton-on-Trent acquired in 1920 (Chapter 2.3).

Crosse and Blackwell built upon the original pickle range by introducing the noted Piccalilli (or Piccalilla as it was first known) as a sauce by Signor Qualliotti in 1832 (above, 4.1). We have noted (above, 4.1) how during this period the firm sourced its pickling onions from East Ham, where hundreds of women were employed to peel them.[118] The 1868 inventory also records how the cellars under 21 Soho Square (building A; Fig 5) contained a pickling vault,[119] with the price list for October 1873 (Fig 39) demonstrating that pickles were filled in jars or casks.[120] The various labels that have survived affixed to the different pots found on this site show that the stoneware bung jars contained Crosse and Blackwell's Piccalilli (<P9>, Fig 35), with the 1868 inventory of their premises noting how Piccalilli was prepared in the Piccalilli room (Fig 47) on the ground floor of the factory of New Building South (building C; Fig 5).[121] The glass assemblage includes 57 rims (77 sherds) from a range of wide-mouthed possible pickle glass bottles. However, as the body can be cylindrical or squared (flat faces were ideal for label fixing), such bottles are difficult to identify from body sherds alone, and it is possible that some of the *c* 600 bases and body sherds recorded as bottle/jar or jar are from pickle bottles.

Although mostly in natural green glass, there are five colourless glass bottles that were probably used for pickles, including one complete example from levelling deposit [34], with a carinated body and a cylindrical neck, decorated with two bands of an oblique Greek key-type pattern in relief (<128>, Fig 48). The rim of a second example of this form was found in the same context, while sherds from a third were present in the fill of the cistern (S7; Chapter 2.1).

'Salad Cream' (product no. 51)

The Crosse and Blackwell illustrated export price list of 1923 shows that a type of salad dressing known as Florence Cream was sold in distinctive long-necked glass bottles, with a body that tapered into a cabled pedestal base and with deep vertical ribbing around the shoulder (Fig 49).[122] Fragments of up to

Fig 49 Florence Cream as advertised in the Crosse and Blackwell export catalogue of 1923 (LMA, 4467/D/01/002, 8, product no. 130)

five mould-blown colourless glass examples that once contained this Florence Cream were found on the site, comprising upper body fragments from two bottles (<124>) and three bases (<126>; 40mm, 44mm and 54mm diameter) from the cistern (S7) fill (Chapter 2.1; Fig 16; Fig 17) and the various underfloor make-up deposits associated with the demolition of the western and north-western arms of the New Building South factory (Chapter 2.1; Fig 5, building C).

'Sauces' (product no. 56)

By the Edwardian period, Crosse and Blackwell produced and sold a large selection of sauces (which included various catsups or ketchups and relishes), sold per dozen in ¼ to ½ pint (0.142 and 0.284 litre) and quart (1.137 litre) bottles.[123] Like the noted pickles (above) some of the names given evoked far-flung places of the globe (Emperor of China and Mogul Sauce); or specifically referenced either the monarchy (eg Royal Table, Prince of Wales Salad Sauce, Payne's Royal Osborne Sauce) or figures closer to home (John Bull and Robert Peel's Sauce).

Sauces were only distributed in glass bottles, not only by Crosse and Blackwell but by all other food manufacturing firms and companies. In the absence of labels, very few of which have survived, or other distinguishing contents markers, and without historical images fragmented bottles are difficult to classify or assign to a particular product from rims or bases alone, but they fall broadly into two types, cylindrical and rectangular. The former were more common on the site, with up to 239 examples having a plain cylindrical body, rounded shoulder and a long narrow neck with a mineral or oil rim finish (<123> and <193>, Fig 50); base diameters range from *c* 39mm to 60mm. Three sauce bottle necks still have corks *in situ*, while one has no cork but the remains of the foil cap (<123> and <193>, Fig 50). With the exception of <122>, all the examples presented in Fig 50 and Fig 53 come from the various levelling deposits associated with New Building South (Chapter 2.1; Fig 5, building C).

One of the main products sold in cylindrical bottles was tomato catsup, which was being made by at least 1846 and is noted in the first of the firm's surviving price lists under 'Tomata Sauce' in ½ pints (0.284 litre) and pints (0.558 litre);[124] during the 1880s it was made for Crosse and Blackwell by the firm Cunnington at Deeping St James, south Lincolnshire, and sent in casks to London from the local railway station, opened by the Great Northern Railway Company in 1848.[125] In 1865 Crosse and Blackwell was said to be producing 27,000 gallons (122,742 litres) of ketchup annually.[126] The wholesale price list for 1910 includes under sauces 'Gordon and Dilworth's Tomato Catsup',[127] a sauce product which is evidenced on site by the two glass stoppers with moulded lettering found (Fig 51, <72> and <117>; Fig 62,

Fig 50 Sauce bottle necks with foil cap, <123>, and cork *in situ*, <193> (scale *c* 1:2)

<123>

<193>

type 1dii <72>). Gordon and Dilworth were catsup producers based in New York, although an advertisement of 1897 shows it was also marketed in England. The advertisement stated that the sauce was 'used by the royal family' and gave a price of 'sixpence and one shilling per bottle', with a contact address of W B Fordham and Sons, York Way, Kings Cross. It is likely that Crosse and Blackwell acted as their distributor in this country. Ketchup bottles usually have a height at least three times greater than the base/body diameter and a relatively long, thin neck to aid pouring; the standard size was 14 fluid oz (0.7 pint or 0.398 litre). Until *c* 1890 ketchup bottles were mouth-blown with a double ring or one part rim finish and sealed with a cork or stopper. After this date they begin to have an externally threaded rim finish to affix a screw cap and by 1910 this was standard.

Fig 51 Glass stoppers <72> and <117> made for Gordon and Dilworth (scale *c* 1:1)

Rectangular bottles are much less common on the site, with fragments from only 21 examples; on most the corners are chamfered, but on four they are rounded. It is unclear how early this form was used; long-necked bottles with flat panels are typical of the period after 1910, but they were probably used well before this (those used for medicines etc are short-necked). Bottles with chamfered corners appear to be associated with two of the most popular products made by Crosse and Blackwell: walnut catsup and mushroom catsup (from at least 1857) – a sauce used to add flavour to fricasseed rabbit, game hash and all kinds of fish. An important find is the near-complete bottle <119> (Fig 52) from one of the underfloor levelling deposits associated with New Building South ([43]; Chapter 2.1; Fig 5, building C), which has part of the original label showing that it contained Mushroom Catsup (recipes for which feature in Eliza Acton's 1845 cookery book) and is identical to an example shown in Crosse and Blackwell's illustrated export price list for 1923.[128] For the making of this product, the mushrooms were gathered from Leicestershire, and 17,000 gallons or 136,000 pints (77,282 litres) of this condiment alone were made in 1857.[129] Another complete bottle of this type from the same underfloor sequence has the initials 'C & B' in relief at the base of one of the main faces, with the letters 'K E' on the underside of the base (<120>, Fig 52), while a third just has 'K E' on the base. While 'C & B'

Fig 52 Glass bottle <119> with label affixed for Mushroom Catsup and similar bottle <120> with moulded initials 'C & B' and 'K E' (scale *c* 1:2)

<121>

<122>

Fig 53 Fluted polygonal sauce, oil or vinegar bottles: <121>, complete (scale *c* 1:2); and base <122> with letters 'C B / M' (scale *c* 1:1)

must refer to Crosse and Blackwell, the significance of 'K E' is unclear; it does not appear to relate to Kilner. Up to 18 other fragmented rectangular bottles, four with rounded corners, may also belong to this group mostly found among the glass.

No examples of the ornate square or polygonal 'gothic' type pepper sauce bottles were found on the site, but one or two narrow-necked square bottles are represented, while a few polygonal fluted bottles in light olive green glass belong to the vertically ribbed category, including a complete example with a packer rim finish (<121>, Fig 53). The base of a larger example has the initials 'CB / M' and some indistinct numbers on the underside (<122>, Fig 53). These elegant bottles may have contained a sauce, oil or vinegar. The style dates from the late 1840s; <121> is made in a three-part mould with a packer rim finish.

'Lea & Perrins Worcestershire Sauce' (product no. 57)

Perhaps the best-known product marketed by Crosse and Blackwell but made elsewhere is Lea and Perrins Worcestershire Sauce, the recipe for which includes anchovies, onions/shallots, molasses, sugar, salt, malt and spirit vinegar, tamarind, soy sauce and various spices. The origin of the sauce is unclear, but it may derive from a local sauce made of anchovies and spices that, as advertised locally in 1830 and 1831, accompanied Worcester lampreys, an eel-like fish.[130]

Lea and Perrins attribute it to a recipe brought back from India by Lord Marcus Sandys,[131] but others point to Captain Henry Lewis Edwardes (1788–1866).[132] Another story is that it was a request for curry powder by Lady Sandys that led to the invention. It is known, however, that the Worcester chemists John Wheeley Lea and William Henry Perrins, partners from 1823, became agents for Johnson's German Sauce in about 1830, when other local chemists Twinberrow and Evans were beginning to market imported Indian sauces.[133] According to the Lea and Perrins story, they were requested to make up a recipe; at first it proved too strong but due to fermentation it mellowed over time and production started in 1837.[134] It was an instant success and by the 1860s Lea and Perrins were selling 300,000 bottles per year.[135]

By 1845 (and possibly since 1843) Crosse and Blackwell became one of the distributing agents for the sauce, bottles of which were by then corked and sealed with Betts's patent metallic capsules (<13>, Fig 54), embossed with the

Fig 54 Lea and Perrins stoppers <77> and <82> (scale *c* 1:1); and Betts's patent foil seal <13> (scale *c* 2:1)

words 'Lea and Perrins Worcestershire Sauce'.[136] The evidence of Crosse and Blackwell's role as distributor of Lea and Perrins Worcestershire Sauce – a product listed separately from its own sauces in the noted 1873 price list (Fig 39)[137] – mainly survives as 56 glass stoppers bearing their moulded lettering (<77> and <82>, Fig 54). From 1895 Worcestershire Sauce was also made by Holbrook and Company, a Birmingham company set up in 1870, one of whose glass stoppers was found on site (<83>, Fig 55), amongst other companies.[138] The standard bottle for this type of sauce is that first made for Lea and Perrins in the 1840s, in natural blue/green glass with a narrow cylindrical body, rounded shoulder and long slightly tapering neck (height usually three to four times greater than diameter). Four of the 239 stratified cylindrical bottles from the site were definitely for this sauce; the most complete, <125>, is dated to the first two decades of the 20th century and has the words 'LEA & PERRINS' in relief-moulded lettering down the side of the bottle and 'C / B / Co /Λ' on the underside.

Fig 55 Glass stopper <83> made for Holbrook and Company (scale *c* 1:1)

'Vinegars' (product no. 67)

Whilst vinegar was a product line in its own right from at least 1840[139] (Chapter 5.2), it was also required for pickling, as it is a strong preservative; the importance of being able to produce and buy in vinegar in the quantities Crosse and Blackwell needed is evidenced by the firm's 1876 acquisition of the vinegar brewery on Brewery and Caledonian Road, Islington, north London (Fig 66). The wholesale price list for January 1910 records vinegar as sold as pure malt vinegar, pure table vinegar and distilled malt vinegar in imperial pints and quarts (0.568 litres and 1.137 litres) (although it does not note the type of container).[140] In addition to the brewery, the infrastructure required for vinegar in the firm's Soho Square complex is recorded in the 1868 inventory of Crosse and Blackwell's premises with the 'Ground Floor of Factory of New Building South' (Chapter 2.1; Fig 5, building C) containing '2 cast iron steam boiling pans 150 gallons [681.90 litres] each, 2 cast iron steam boiling pans 100 gallons [454.60 litres] each, steam jackets, safety valves set in brickwork, oak vinegar steam boiling round gauge 250 gallons [1136.50 litres] with brick piers under piped in. Platinum steam coil, vinegar slate tank, passing

Fig 56 Stopper <98>
and foil <194> from
Sarson's vinegar bottles
(scale *c* 1:1)

<98>

<194>

tubs, sieves'.[141] Whilst we do not know what the various upright bottles (<P4>–<P6>, Fig 34) supplied extensively by C I C Bailey's Fulham stoneware pothouse were used for on this site, it is likely they were put to use as the containers of the vinegar and the corrosive acids/chemicals required on the factory floor. The material evidence of Crosse and Blackwell's vinegar making is otherwise limited to a glass stopper with foil cap and part of another (<98> and <194>, Fig 56) found in the various underfloor make-up deposits associated with the demolition of the western and north-western arms of the New Building South factory (Chapter 2.1; Fig 5, building C). The stopper and cap are related to Sarson's vinegar, a London brand founded by Thomas Sarson in 1794 in Shoreditch, Hackney, and a product that in 2015 survives as a brand manufactured by the Japanese vinegar manufacturer Mizkan.

4.3 Sealing and stoppering

A critical element in Crosse and Blackwell's operation was the effective sealing and stoppering of their food products in an airtight container in order to best preserve their contents. Stoppers fit inside the neck of the container, while lids or caps fit on or over the mouth; most closures found on the site fall into the category of stoppers, but the larger glass examples used for jars are here defined as lids. Thousands of glass bottle stoppers were found on the site (below), but the archaeological evidence of how the various other pots and glass jars were sealed remains limited.

The oldest ways of sealing bottles and jars were with covers of leather, parchment or textile, sometimes sealed with clay, wax or lead, or mixes of wax and resin used as plugs. The plain cylindrical and vertically grooved refined white earthenware (REFW) jars found would have been 'tied down' with paper or parchment, but the site yielded no evidence of this known practice.

Cork stoppers, made of the bark of the cork oak tree (*Quercus suber* and *Quercus occidentalis*), were first introduced to England in the 16th century and soon became popular for two main reasons: cork is inert and so does not react with the contents it is sealing; and it is also elastic, being compressible when dry but expanding when wet, thus making a tight seal possible for vessels of all sizes. Usually held in place by a wire of some sort, their use increased in the 17th century and they remained popular until the 1920s. There were, however, disadvantages – such as time taken to fit a cork without breaking the bottle, the difficulty in removing it intact so that the bottle could be resealed and the practice of steaming bottles shut which caused the cork to expand heightened the risk of breakage. This led to the introduction of glass and rubber stoppers (both, like cork, inert materials), which largely replaced corks as production of machine-made bottles increased during the 20th century, although many closures used a combination of glass and cork. Corks are still used for wine bottles and glass for some jar lids, but both have now been largely replaced by other types of seal.

In 1870 the firm entered into an agreement with James Winter who 'has provisionally registered several inventions for filling and corking or stoppering bottles and jars in vacuum by machinery the patents for which he as [sic] not proceeded with'.[142] For the sum of £50, Winter sold his rights to these inventions to the firm and the agreement stipulated he worked with 'an engineer in Crosse and Blackwell's premises to install the machine' and would be paid 'another £100 after it has been finished and found to be in good working order'. Through the fitting of this machine to fill and cork bottles in vacuum and its operation by an experienced workman, the firm hoped it would 'reduce the breakage of glass bottles and the loss of contents which arise from the ordinary method of steaming'.[143]

The most popular method, nevertheless, of sealing the glass jars, the English brown salt-glazed stoneware (ENGS) and stoneware with Bristol glaze (ENGS BRST) upright bottles, mustard and bung jars and the similar plain shouldered refined white earthenware (REFW) vessels was the tightly fitted cork sealed with wax; some of the stoneware mustard jars (<P42> and <P43>, Fig 57) and a few glass bottles (<193>, Fig 50) were still sealed in this way. Whilst only 13 smaller corks for glass bottles have survived loose, 86 disc-shaped cork bungs

Fig 57 English stoneware with Bristol glaze mustard jars with cork stoppers, <P42> and <P43>, and food jars, <P44>–<P46> (scale *c* 1:2)

Fig 58 Cork bung jar stoppers <106>, <107> and <142> (scale *c* 1:2)

<106>

<107>

<142>

(742g) were recovered from the underfloor levelling deposits ([34], [36] and [43]) associated with the demolition of the western and north-western arms of the New Building South factory (Chapter 2.1; Fig 5, building C) and from [19], one of the cistern (S7; Fig 16; Fig 17) fills, and would have been used to stopper and seal Crosse and Blackwell's pottery and glass jars. Most of these bungs fall into two sizes: 52–59mm and 60–65mm in diameter (38 and 43 examples respectively). The main cluster, however, measures 58–63mm diameter (58 examples; <106>, Fig 58), with three at 65–66mm diameter; only two are larger than this, with diameters of *c* 95mm and 94 x 97mm (<107>, Fig 58). Thickness is 13–25mm, with most examples measuring *c* 16–22mm. Most are more or less straight-sided, but some are more bevelled and three have a central perforation (<142>, Fig 58), presumably to insert a form of knop to enable the lifting of the lid; two others have semi-finished perforations. All the corks appear to have been used and some are blackened on one or both surfaces, but there is no evidence that they were associated with any wires or sealed in any way.

Crosse and Blackwell also used composite corks, represented by 11 examples combining a conventional cork (17mm and 20mm diameter, exposed length *c* 22–25mm) with moulded disc heads made of fine agglomerated cork, a compound invented *c* 1890 and sometimes made with added clay. All heads have milled sides/edges with a hollow underside, and were secured by an integral pin embedded in the cork; most now have a gap between the two where the cork has shrunk. The seven stoppers from the cistern (S7) fill [19] (four illustrated; <96>, Fig 59) are 26–31mm in diameter, while the two (<16>,

<109>

Fig 59 Cork and cork compound stoppers <96>, with coat of arms and 'Crosse & Blackwell' branding, and octagonal stopper <109> with 'C & B' logo (scale *c* 1:1)

<96>

<52>) from underfloor levelling deposits [36] (Chapter 2.1; Fig 5, building C) associated with the demolition of the western and north-western arm of the New Building South warehouse and factory are 31mm in diameter. All have the same moulded design identifying and advertising the Crosse and Blackwell brand. Also found in cistern fill [19] are two larger stoppers (one illustrated; <109>, Fig 59) with shank diameters of 25mm (exposed length 19mm); the moulded straight-sided octagonal heads are 37mm across and have the letters 'C & B' above and below the royal arms within a central roundel. Three further large cork compound stoppers, all round-topped with milled edges, are identified by their moulded lettering as products of Mellin's infant food, a business based at the Marlborough Works, Peckham, Southwark, from *c* 1870.

Also found on the site were 18 ceramic discs from composite closures that probably involved an iron clip-on cover, all of which were from the underfloor make-up deposits, [36], associated with the demolition of the western and north-western arm of the New Building South warehouse and factory (Chapter 2.1; Fig 5, building C). All are from patent hermetic sealed lids and metal closures made by the likes of the Fulham pothouse[144] and presented in Doulton and Watt's illustrated catalogue of 1873 as 'Registered air-tight covered jars for pickling and preserving', for use on stoneware 'food jars', such as <P44>–<P46> (Fig 57).[145] The discs fall into four different types, but all are of the same general construction, consisting of a flat-based, flat-topped ceramic disc with bevelled sides and a central pin made of a dark silvery metal, mainly lead with some zinc;[146] in every case a white powdery substance survives around the pin. In most cases the pin is incomplete, but on the five intact examples it projects for *c* 6mm and has an expanded round base with stamped lettering (variously 'D' or 'O': <37>; 'A' (possibly preceded by 'H'): <38>; 'JG': <66>; and 'Y &': <197>).

In addition there are the glass closures, comprising lids and stoppers, which had an advantage over metal ones as, being inert, they did not affect the taste of the contents. In the case of glass lids, a tight seal would have been achieved by either fitting the lids over a cork or using a rubber gasket. In all, 39 examples (2.952kg) of glass lids were found on the site, all made of natural green glass. Examples of the three types of plain glass lids are shown in Fig 60; examples of a fourth lid type, with a recessed centre and relief-moulded lettering around the edge, are shown in Fig 33.

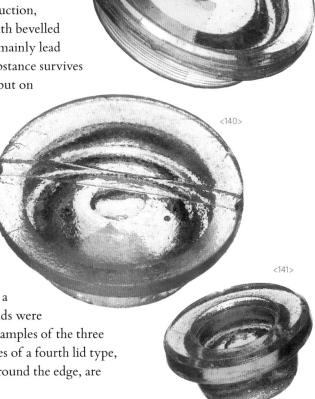

Fig 60 Plain glass lids: type 1 – flat-topped, plain <139>; type 2 – flat-topped plain with a groove across the centre <140>; and type 3 – plain with a recessed centre <141> (scale *c* 1:1)

<139>

<140>

<141>

The most common closure, and by far the largest single component of the glass assemblage, is the glass stopper found in quantities that far outstrip the numbers of food sauce bottles they were once intended for. In all, there are some 4410 examples (*c* 85kg), mainly from the various underfloor make-up deposits (in particular [36]) associated with the demolition of the western and north-western arm of the New Building South warehouse and factory (Chapter 2.1; Fig 5, building C), of which a sample has been retained after being recorded. Most are natural green glass, reflecting the colour of the bottles they were designed for, but a few are in natural blue or colourless glass and are plain, although some have relief-moulded numbers or lettering, as outlined below.

Stoppers comprise two or three components: the shank, the neck (rare in this assemblage) and the head (also known as the finial). Here, six different stopper designs or types (types 1–6: Figs 61–3) were identified and all but one of the complete first two (types 1–2) have shanks with the remains of a cracked-off sprue/pontil; the only exception is <86>, the end of which has been ground. If this was the intention for all stoppers, those found on site were either unfinished or destined for cheaper products or outlets. For bottles intended for use with liquids, an exact airtight seal could be achieved by grinding the stopper shank and the bore of the bottle neck to make a perfect fit; this process made such bottles at least twice as expensive as bottles without stoppers.[147] Unground stoppers were generally used for dry goods, but could be made airtight by adding a cork collar (shell-cork) to the upper part of the tapering shank, or by adding a screw thread.

A more detailed account of the six stopper types is provided in an archive report summarised here.[148] Most stoppers from the site fall into the type 1 group, mostly of natural green glass, with added cork collar (<110>, Fig 61). The depth of the latter would have been dictated by the size of the bottle and the type of finish, but where it survives it is *c* 10–11mm deep, designed to fit a bottle with oil or mineral rim finish with an internal ledge, or cork rest, inside the bore of the neck *c* 12mm below the mouth, although they could have been used with other finishes if the bore was the correct size (<55>, Fig 61). There has been some debate as to whether the cork was intended to stay *in situ* once fitted into the bottle neck, with the glass shank passing through it whenever it was inserted or removed, or whether the two were intended to travel together. The evidence from the Crosse and Blackwell site does not help answer this as none of the complete bottle necks have any cork rings inside them, and although many stoppers still have the cork sheath it can be argued that all were discarded before they were used.

Fig 61 Club Sauce glass and shell-cork stopper (type 1) <110>, and stoppers with foil caps <55> and <15>, the latter with raised lettering outlined in red 'D. COUTTS & Cᵒ LONDON' and 'OLD YET FIRM / REGISTERED' above an oak tree trade mark (scale *c* 1:1)

While most type 1 stoppers have a simple flat or convex head, some have relief-moulded lettering relating them to Lea and Perrins or other manufacturers. More interesting is the presence of numbers on the upper or underside of the head, with '6' by far the most common (2344 stoppers), followed by '14' (122 examples); others include '4', '5', '8', '34', '& / 11', 'C / 14', 'O / 14' and 'T / 14'. Some stoppers have the remains of an embossed metal foil cover with the Crosse and Blackwell name and address over the head (<55>, Fig 61), and it seems likely that this was intended for all such stoppers; the largest, <11>, for a pickle jar, measures *c* 40mm in diameter. The cap appears to have extended over the underside of the head, suggesting that it was intended to stay in place and not be removed as part of the process of opening the bottle; no stoppers have an intact cap and a cork sheath, but white deposits left by the cap and the fact that there is a gap of 1mm between the cork and the head/finial suggest that two were used together, logically with the cap applied first. Examples with slipped or damaged caps from one of the underfloor deposits may be rejects. Also present is a foil-capped stopper with lettering picked out in red reading 'D. COUTTS & C° (arch) / LONDON (inverted arch)', and at the centre 'OLD YET FIRM (arch) / REGISTERED (inverted arch)' above and below an oak tree flanked by 'TRADE' and 'MARK' (<15>, Fig 61).

Other variations on the standard type 1 stoppers include examples with opposed pairs of ridges or guide lines that may have been intended to hold a wire in place (<74>, Fig 62). Others are made in a two-part mould and are designed to give a better grip, either with ridges around a straight-sided head (<84>, Fig 62), or milled (<99>, Fig 62) or lobed (<100>, Fig 62), respectively. Most have smooth seams, but one is poorly cast (<73>, Fig 63). Some type 1 stoppers have lettering on the slightly concave or recessed upper surface (<72>, Fig 62), but many are quite plain (<95>, Fig 62), as are the rare stoppers with straight-sided shanks (<102>, Fig 62).

A further five different glass stopper types (2–6) were also identified. First among this group (type 2) is the screw thread glass stopper, dated from 1861 to the late 1870s in America[149] and possibly used for mineral water or other effervescent liquids, rather than foodstuffs. The screw threads can be either clockwise or anti-clockwise, while the heads are lobed (<71>, Fig 63) or milled (<73>, Fig 63). Most are in colourless glass and made in a two-part mould; the forms follow the same pattern as type 1 (above), but are more limited. The ridged glass stopper (type 3), whilst similar to <100> (Fig 62), is smaller, with a lobed wall and two upwardly bevelled horizontal threads around the shank instead of a spiral. One example has the words '/REGISTERED / JULY 1881/' around the edge and '/N° 6434 /' at the centre (<69>, Fig 63), the other reads '/ Registered No 6454/' around the edge. Fourth (type 4) is a glass stopper patented by the glasshouse of Rylands in Barnsley: this is flat-topped, made in a two-part mould with the words 'RYLANDS PATENT' around the edge

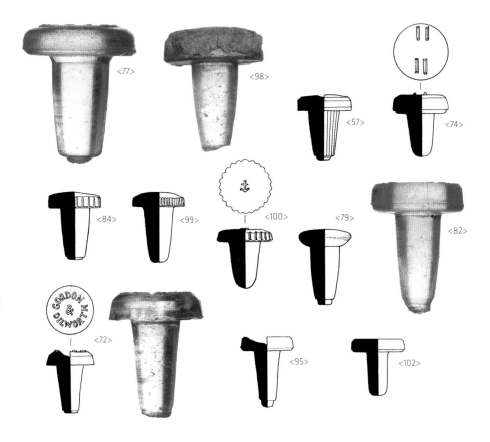

Fig 62 Type 1 glass stoppers: 1ai – flat head with lettering <77> and convex head with foil cap <98>; 1aii – plain with fluted shank <57>; 1aiii – plain head with opposed guidelines <74>; 1bi – ribbed head <84>; 1bii – milled head <99>; 1biii – lobed head <100>; 1ci – bi-convex head <79>; 1di – slightly concave head with lettering <82>; 1dii – recessed head with lettering <72>; 1diii – plain concave head <95>; and 1ei – flat head with straight-sided shank <102> (scale 1:2, photographs 1:1)

and an expanded terminal to the shank (<76>, Fig 63). The final two glass stoppers (types 5 and 6) are with finials. Type 5 is made of colourless glass with a ground straight-sided shank and raised rectangular knop handle (<104>, not illustrated). Finally, there are the two large stoppers/lids (type 6) made of colourless glass with a ground shank and raised rectangular knop handle (<105>, not illustrated). The underside is hollow with two interlinked hearts in relief on the flat surface, while the tops are etched with the numbers '254' and '918'.

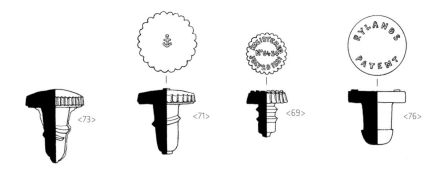

Fig 63 Types 2–4 glass stoppers: 2bii – screw thread, poorly cast milled head <73>; 2biii – screw thread, lobed head <71>; 3 – horizontal thread, ridged head <69>; and 4 – Rylands patent glass stopper, expanded terminal to the shank and flat-topped head <76> (scale 1:2)

Notes to Chapter 4

1 Ehrman 1999, 69

2 LMA, 4467/E/01/005, *Group News*, 7

3 LMA, 4467/G/03/002, A chat about preserved foods, *Irish Social Rev*, 4 May 1907, 56

4 LMA 4467/A/01/002

5 LMA, 4467/A/03/001, 7 footnote 1, letter from Richard S___, 18 December 1832

6 LMA, 4467/A/03/001, 7 footnote 2, letter from Richard S___, 18 December 1832

7 LMA, 4467/A/03/001, letter from Richard S___, 18 December 1832, letter from Annabel, 12 July 1851

8 Atkins 2013, 44; also Shurtleff and Akiko 2012, 170

9 LMA 4467/A/01/002; LMA 4467/C/01/002; LMA 4467/C/01/004

10 LMA 4467/C/01/002

11 LMA, 4467/C/01/001

12 LMA, 4467/C/01/003

13 For 1846 and 1873: LMA 4467/G/03/002, 105, 177–8

14 LMA 4467/G/03/002, 105

15 LMA, 4467/E/01/005, *Group News*, 7

16 Atkins 2013, 46

17 Ibid, 47

18 Ibid, 48

19 LMA, 4467/A/03/001, 15, letter to Reginald, 26 August 1860

20 LMA 4467/E/01/003, Fruit growing in Spain, *Square Mag*, May–June 1920

21 LMA, 4467/G/03/002, 75, newspaper cutting from *Public Health*, February 1908

22 Atkins 2013, 45

23 LMA 4467/A/03/001, 15–16 footnote 2, letter to Reginald, 26 August 1860

24 LMA, 4467/A/03/001, 15 footnote 1, letter to Reginald, 26 August 1860

25 Tames 2003, 81

26 LMA, 4467/G/03/002, 162, offprint of *Leisure Hour*, 1860

27 LMA, 4467/A/03/001, 7

footnote 1, letter from Mr Richard S___, 18 December 1832

28 LMA, 4467/G/03/003/ A, 75, newspaper cutting from *Public Health*, February 1908

29 LMA, 4467/G/03/003/ A, newspaper cutting from *Daily Mail*, 26 February 1921

30 LMA 4467/G/03/003/A, 2

31 Hartley 2011, 47, 51

32 LMA 4467/E/01/003, Not a days illness, *Square Mag*, September 1920, 21

33 LMA, 4467/G/03/002, 162, offprint of *Leisure Hour*, 1860

34 LMA, 4467/F/02/004

35 *Bryan Donkin*

36 Ibid

37 *J S J* 1961, 21

38 *J S J* 1957, 18

39 LMA, 4467/C/02/002

40 LMA 4467/C/02/002, 1–5

41 LMA, 4467/C/02/002, 37

42 LMA, 4467/C/02/002, 48–51

43 LMA, 4467/C/02/002, 30–1

44 LMA, 4467/C/02/002, 13

45 LMA, 4467/C/02/002, 25

46 LMA, 4467/C/02/002, 15

47 LMA, 4467/C/02/002, 23–4

48 LMA, 4467/C/02/002, 18–19

49 LMA, 4467/C/02/002, 20–1

50 LMA, 4467/C/02/002, 17

51 LMA, 4467/C/02/002, 26

52 LMA, 4467/C/02/002, 27

53 LMA, 4467/C/02/002, 29

54 LMA, 4467/C/02/002, 32–4

55 *J S J* 1993, 19

56 LMA, 4467/G/03/002, Oxtail soup: interesting action, *Cork Examiner*, 22 April 1904, 8

57 LMA, 4467/G/03/002, [various newspaper cuttings], 41–4

58 LMA, 4467/G/03/002, 110, Food fraud, *Mrs Bull*, 5 November 1910

59 LMA, 4467/D/01/001, 11

60 Atkins 2013, 43

61 Creswick 1987; Lockhart et al nd, 55–8

62 *Glassmaking*

63 Atkins 2013, 43

64 *South Larnarkshire [RG.1978.485.a]*

65 LMA, 4467/D/01/001, 2–12

66 LMA, 4467/D/01/001, 3

67 LMA, 4467/D/01/001, 8

68 LMA, 4467/D/01/001, 4

69 *ILN*, 11 February 1922, 201

70 LMA, 4467/D/01/001, 5

71 LMA 4467/D/01/001, 3, 5

72 LMA, 4467/D/01/001, 3

73 LMA, 4467/E/01/003, Not a days illness, *Square Mag*, September 1920, 21

74 Hartley 2011, 54

75 Green 1999, fig 130 stamps H, J, K and M

76 Askey 1998, 127

77 Ibid, 148–52

78 Green 1999, 169

79 Ibid

80 Ibid, 365–8

81 Ibid, 361–4

82 Ibid, 365, form 419

83 Ibid, forms 403–4

84 Ibid, form 426

85 Ibid, form 421

86 Ibid, 171, form 425

87 LMA, 4467/D/01/001, 9, product no. 63

88 Green 1999, 159, eg fig 134, types 388–9

89 LMA, 4467/D/01/001, 2–11

90 LMA, 4467/G/03/002, 105

91 LMA, 4467/G/03/002, 187–8

92 LMA, 4467/D/01/001

93 LMA, 4467/G/03/002, 187–8

94 LMA, 4467/D/01/001

95 LMA, 4467/D/01/002

96 LMA, 4467/D/01/002, 4, product no. 73

97 LMA, 4467/D/01/002, 8, product no. 130

98 LMA, 4467/F/02/004

99 LMA, 4467/D/01/001, 2–12

100 LMA, 4467/D/01/001, 4

101 LMA, 4467/G/03/002, 187–8

102 Valenze 2011, 170

103 *J S J* 1993, 18

104 LMA, 4467/F/02/004

105 LMA, 4467/D/01/001, 2–12

106 LMA, 4467/D/01/001, 7

107 LMA, 4467/A/03/001, 10–11

108 LMA, 4467/E/01/003, Three generations, *Square Mag*, September 1920, 23

109 *J S J* 1957, 14

110 LMA, 4467/D/01/002, 17, 19

111 LMA, 4467/D/01/002, 21

112 *Maling history*

113 Mathew 2000, 6

114 LMA, 4467/D/01/002, 47, product no. 940

115 Copeland 1990

116 LMA, 4467/D/01/001, 8

117 *J S J* 1957, 13

118 LMA, 4467/A/03/001, 15–16, letter to Reginald, 26 August 1860

119 LMA, 4467/F/02/004

120 LMA 4467/G/03/002, 187–8

121 LMA, 4467/F/02/004

122 LMA 4467/D/01/002, 8, product no. 130

123 LMA, 4467/D/01/001, 8, product no. 56

124 LMA 4467/G/03/002, 105

125 *Preserves*

126 Mayhew 1865, 174–88 referenced in Atkins 2013, 46

127 LMA, 4467/D/01/001, 8, product no. 56; also *Advert for Gordon and Dilworth*

128 Acton 1845, 132–4; LMA, 4467/D/01/002, product no. 73

129 LMA, 4467/G/03/002, 162, offprint of *Leisure Hour*, 1860

130 Docio 2013; *Worcester*

131 Atkins 2013, 44

132 Jones 1997

133 *Worcester*

134 *Lea & Perrins*

135 Atkins 2013, 44

136 Shurtleff and Akiko 2012, 8

137 LMA 4467/G/03/002, 187–8

138 Shurtleff and Akiko 2012, 9; Keogh 1997

139 LMA, 4467/E/01/006

140 LMA, 4467/D/01/001, 10, product no. 67

141 LMA, 4467/F/02/004

142 LMA 4467/C/01/007

143 LMA 4467/C/01/007

144 LMA 4467/C/01/007, 171

145 Similar to Green 1999, 171, form 425

146 Becker 2014

147 *Bottle closures*

148 Blackmore and Jeffries 2014

149 Ibid

CHAPTER 5

SALES AND MARKETING: HOME AND ABROAD

5.1 Marketing

Edmund Crosse and Thomas Blackwell quickly moved to gain their first royal appointment from the newly crowned Queen Victoria in 1837[1] and were able to cement their position and ambition as the food manufacturers of choice for the upper and middle classes through the unprecedented employment endorsements of their various products by the celebrity chefs of their era, Signor Qualliotti, Alexis Soyer and Charles Emile Francatelli (Chapter 4.1). A later descendent of Edmund, Victor Crosse, nevertheless suggests through his access to the Lord Steward's department that a royal warrant for trading with the royal household had been held by West and Wyatt since 1762.[2] In 1868 they added to their British royal warrant both the patronage of and contract as suppliers and provider of goods to the Ministry of the Home of Emperor Napoleon[3] and the king of Belgium.[4]

The 1873 price lists for the London (Lambeth) stoneware manufacturers of James Stiff and Sons and Doulton and Watts advertised a paper-labelling service with price determined by measurement size per dozen.[5] Only a few of the affixed paper labels that once advertised the contents of the various ceramic and glass jars and bottles found on the site have survived (Fig 35; Fig 45). However, the first of Crosse and Blackwell's illustrated export price lists (from 1923)[6] demonstrates that the packaging and labelling of their product range was an integral part of their sales strategy and was a practice adopted since at least 1864, when Henry Mayhew, who included Crosse and Blackwell in his *The shops and companies of London: Volume 1* survey (published 1865) records that labels were applied to nine million of their bottles and pots in that year.[7] When Mayhew was undertaking this survey the process was carried out at 20 Soho Square, which once housed the export labelling department (Fig 9), with the 1868 inventory[8] noting that the second floor of 20 Soho Square (area N: Chapter 2.1; Fig 5, building B; Fig 8; Fig 10) stocked a number of brushes for labelling.

The paper labels project a number of important messages. First, the emphasis on declaring the purity of their food products was a response to the requirements of the Adulteration of Food, Drink and Drugs Act of 1872 which made it an offence to sell food products without contents being declared to the purchaser by the manufacturer (discussion of food adulteration: Chapter

6.1). In addition to advertising the contents of the tin, pot, glass or packet, the branding of goods with their name reinforced the link between the consumer and manufacturer. Labelling also allowed the firm to display their various awards, with the 'Grand medal progress, the highest honor gained for good products to any British Exhibitor was awarded by the jurors of the Vienna Universal Exhibition' representing just one success.[9] Crosse and Blackwell, therefore, presented the image of a food manufacturer that could be trusted and through the firm's acquirement of a royal appointment, the highest accolade afforded to a retailer, it also projected an air of exclusivity. The various labels applied to the refined white earthenware (REFW) jars found on this site advertise Crosse and Blackwell as purveyors of foods to 'His Majesty the King' (either Edward VII (1901–10) or George V (1910–36)). Whilst the endorsement was uncontroversial in the United Kingdom, by 1917 the company was forced to acknowledge the objections of a number of countries – in particular Australia – to the use of the royal warrant on Crosse and Blackwell's products. A number of correspondences by the director, Mr Francis Samuel Blackwell, have survived documenting the decision by the company to first replace the words royal warrant with royal appointment[10] before it agreed that royal warrant could remain, but for use for the home, not export, market.[11]

The company, therefore, used a range of different marketing techniques to advertise its wares and project its image. In addition to the carefully worded labels affixed to its products, we have noted how they used monthly price lists from at least 1846 (Fig 38; Chapter 4.2) to distribute to its wholesalers and stockists, and to further promote its wares. Among the printed ephemera, a poster (Fig 64) made in 1916 neatly captures how the company projected its global reach and position as a leading food manufacturer, even during the stresses placed on it by the First World War (Chapter 6.2).

5.2 Transport and export market

The Crosse and Blackwell company was unusual for its day in its ability to successfully integrate the roles of wholesaler, distributor and manufacturer, and their expansion was due in part to their ability to take advantage of those 'Victorian technologies' of 'canning, the steamship, railways and refrigeration'.[12] How they stored and transported their range of food products across the globe is considered here, but the decision to sell their products worldwide appears to have been made a decade or so after the firm's foundation, with its first export order sent in February 1840 to Captain Daniel Warren in Calcutta (modern-day Kolkata, India), diligently recorded and preserved as follows:[13]

20 Cases, each 3 doz [dozen] of Bottled Fruits
9 Cases of Sauce

20 Cases of Pickles, each 1-doz.qts [1 dozen quarts]

1 Case of Capers, pts [pints]

2 Cases of Mustard

2 Cases, each 3-doz, pts. [3 dozen pints], Salad Oil

8 Cases Vinegar, each containing 6-doz Qts [6 dozen quarts]

3 doz Anchovies (Please note this in stouter bottles and longer necks)

Thomas Blackwell and Edmund Crosse therefore had a keen eye for the emerging global markets and during the following decade many of their new product lines made specific reference to Britain's colonies as a marketing

Fig 64 Poster advertising Crosse and Blackwell's export price list, dated April 1916, with illustrations of their premises
(LMA, 4467/G/03/002, 291–2)

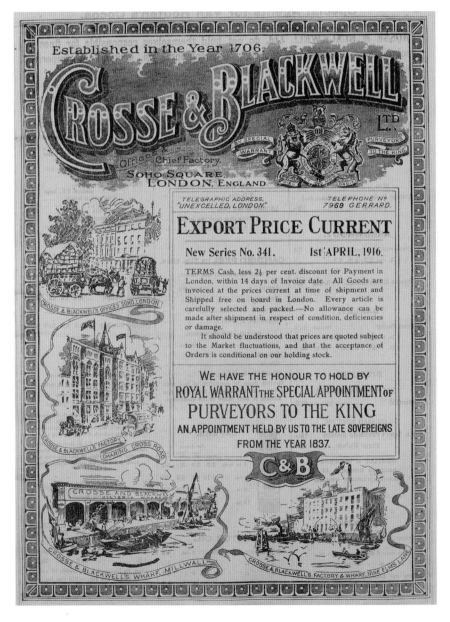

technique. For example Oriental Sauce was on offer 'to late residents of India and other hot climates'[14] and many of their other products also spoke to the settlers of Britain's burgeoning colonial territories, with names such as the noted (Chapter 4.1) Abdool Fygo's Chutney and Mulligatawny Pastes.

Logistics were clearly an important consideration for Crosse and Blackwell as the ingredients for their products were sourced from London markets, the market gardens of Fulham, the South Downs (Hampshire and Sussex) and the orchards of Surrey, Kent and beyond (Chapter 4.1). Whilst the evidence in the company's archive for how it distributed its products throughout the United Kingdom is, at best, only occasionally and implicitly referred to, it does appear, however, to have used horse and cart in London right up to its removal to Branston in 1921 (Fig 65).[15] The evidence of how the firm developed its export market has survived better.

Fig 65 View down Sutton Street looking west towards Soho Square showing a line of Crosse and Blackwell horse and carts loading or unloading into their premises
(LMA, 4467/C/03/003, 220, *Square Mag*, February 1920, 4)

The buildings and infrastructure required by the firm to facilitate its export trade can be seen in its acquisition in 1862 of the first Thameside premises on the north bank of the River Thames at Victoria Wharf (Fig 66), located on Earl Street and Upper Thames Street[16] just to the east of Blackfriars Bridge and to the east of Puddle Dock in the Baynard Warde.[17] Earl Street continued into Upper Thames Street and, in the various references to the Crosse and Blackwell site in the documentary sources, it is often listed as being on Upper Thames Street. After the riverside area to the west of Blackfriars Bridge was removed for the formation of Victoria Embankment (in 1865, completed 1870) the firm made the first of its commissions with the architect R L Roumieu, who designed the wharf building,[18] but it seems probable that the Upper Thames Street wharfs and warehouses and Roumieu's building survived till after the Second World War. The inventory description of 1868[19] for Victoria Wharf implies a large four-storey riverside building, with warehousing space. Little or no manufacturing or processing equipment is listed. However, there are numerous mentions of lifts, loading shoots, cranes, jibs and hooks, which

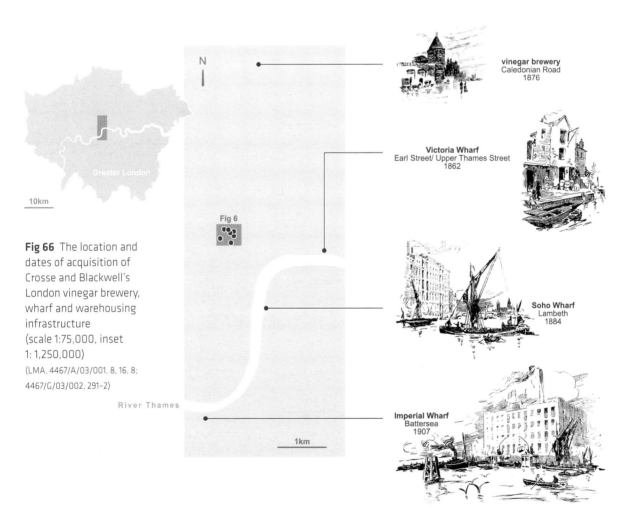

Fig 66 The location and dates of acquisition of Crosse and Blackwell's London vinegar brewery, wharf and warehousing infrastructure (scale 1:75,000, inset 1:1,250,000)
(LMA, 4467/A/03/001, 8, 16, 8; 4467/G/03/002, 291–2)

vinegar brewery
Caledonian Road
1876

Victoria Wharf
Earl Street/ Upper Thames Street
1862

Soho Wharf
Lambeth
1884

Imperial Wharf
Battersea
1907

indicate the loading of large heavy items on to river barges for transportation. The firm opened its first factory abroad in 1864 in Morrison's Quay, Cork, Ireland,[20] for tinning and exporting salmon caught from the River Shannon.[21] It was described as the first of its kind in the world.

By 1865, Henry Mayhew presents the firm as having already obtained a significant global reach, and noted its main export markets as India, China and Australia,[22] with southern Africa, Canada and New Zealand also featuring. The capital gains of these ventures can be witnessed in the company's annual statement of trade which record exports of £146,380 in 1852 rising to £435,194 in 1870, with the empire accounting for 60–69% of Crosse and Blackwell's exports between 1860 and 1890.[23] The challenges in building and sustaining a successful export market in terms of packaging and preservation of their foods and transportation, during the early history of the company, must have nevertheless been significant. Insights are presented in the *Square Magazine* with an article recording the retirement of the company's export manager, Mr E S Wyatt.[24] Though he had held this title since 1905, he had worked at the business for 49 years. The article records how when he started working (in 1871) Crosse and Blackwell used 'Wheatley's Overland Express through which we used to send small consignments of ham, bacon and cheese to India. The goods were carried on the back of camels through the desert and were over two months in reaching Madras and Calcutta …'. The firm sent exports to India, China and Japan via boats that 'left about once every month, and to Australia and New Zealand about every two months, but the United States was served about every three months'.[25]

As we have seen, by the 1870s the firm seemed no longer content to adapt existing buildings, but preferred to commission purpose-built buildings around their central site at Soho Square (Chapter 2.1; Fig 5). Instead of manufacturing pickles and sauces in cramped and awkward spaces that had not been built for the purpose, the efficiency, ease and especially the fire safety aspects of designed factory and warehouse buildings were benefits the firm could now afford. Moving this function from Stacey Street (Chapter 2.1; Fig 6) in 1884, Crosse and Blackwell's first purpose-built premises now enabled the manufacture of export pickles by the Thames at Soho Wharf, Lambeth, at 'the (southern) end of the Westminster Bridge' (Fig 66) before this building was cleared for the construction of a London County Council building in the first decade of the 20th century.[26] Soho Wharf was replaced by the newer and more substantial waterside premises at Nine Elms Wharf, Battersea – Imperial Wharf – in 1907 (Fig 66). This was the largest riverside site occupied by the firm and the building was again arranged around a central courtyard with two cranes over the river. Whilst *The Times* newspaper reported that at the turn of the 20th century Crosse and Blackwell employed their own lightermen to transport their goods up and down the Thames,[27] a year after it opened, Imperial Wharf benefited from delivery of the motor barge *Mirabella* (Fig 67) to carry cargo and tow barges to the Tilbury docks in the Thames estuary in a one-day round trip, during which it carried exports such as jams and pickles and returned with sugar and similar goods.[28]

In 1910 the establishment of further salmon canneries in British Columbia, western Canada, and in Baltimore, on the east coast of the United States, further expanded Crosse and Blackwell's capacity in tinned salmon, which led to the final closure of their Morrison's Quay plant in Ireland (an event hastened by a number of strikes that had hit the factory in 1902[29]). By the 1920s, selling their products across the world was facilitated by sole representatives or agents which Crosse and Blackwell employed[30] and at the point of their move from Soho to Branston, begun in 1921, the 'Marking a record' article in the *Square Magazine* boasts 'sales over the world were a record in the history of the Company' for that year.[31] In 1920 the company used the aeroplane to transport its products for the first time to the Continent (Fig 68).[32]

The demands and importance of maintaining and growing their export market appear to have been the primary motive for Crosse and Blackwell's move to the Branston factory, completed by 1921;[33] the *Evening News* in 1920 quoted an unsourced member of the company who explained how the savings 'in packing, loading and unloading, and freightage would be very large'.[34]

Fig 67 Photograph of the motor barge *Mirabella* (LMA, 4467/G/03/003, 184)

CROSSE AND BLACKWELL 1830–1921

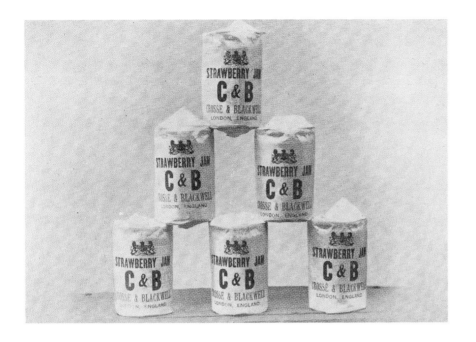

Fig 68 Stack of specially wrapped and branded ceramic jam jars celebrating Crosse and Blackwell's first use of the aeroplane to transport its products to the Continent, depicted in a 1920 edition of the *Square Magazine* (LMA, 4467/E/01/003, August 1920, 9)

Notes to Chapter 5

1 LMA, 4467/E/01/005, 7

2 LMA, 4467/A/02/005

3 LMA, 4467/A/01/004

4 LMA, 4467/A/01/005. Observations by Kristiaan De Vlamynck (pers comm) have shown how many of Crosse and Blackwell's stoneware pots have survived in Belgium in 2015, through his study of private collections and visits to second-hand markets here. Vessels which carry both the maker's stamp of George Skey of Wilnecote (Tamworth, Staffordshire/ Warwickshire) and 'C&B' proprietary stamp (eg <P15>, Fig 36) often feature.

5 Green 1999, 364, 368

6 LMA, 4467/D/01/002

7 Atkins 2013, 46

8 LMA, 4467/F/02/004

9 LMA, 4467/A/01/003

10 LMA, 4467/G/03/003, 43–4

11 LMA, 4467/G/03/003, 85–6, 23 May 1917

12 Tames 2003, 7

13 LMA, 4467/E/01/006

14 Atkins 2013, 46

15 LMA, 4467/G/03/003/A, 140, newspaper cutting from *Evening News*, 24 February 1920

16 LMA, 4467/A/03/001, 6, 16 footnote 4

17 Harben 1918

18 *Builder* 1877, 691

19 LMA, 4467/F/02/004

20 LMA, 4467/A/03/001, 17 footnote 1

21 LMA, 4467/E/01/005, 7

22 Mayhew 1865, 174–88 referenced in Atkins 2013, 46

23 Atkins 2013, 46

24 LMA, 4467/E/01/003, Known all over the world, retirement of Mr E S Wyatt, *Square Mag*, January–March 1921, 4–5

25 LMA, 4467/E/01/003, Known all over the world, retirement of Mr E S Wyatt, *Square Mag*, January–March 1921, 5

26 LMA, 4467/A/03/001, 18–19

27 *The Times*, Thames lightermen's strike, 27 October 1900, 13

28 LMA, 4467/G/03/002, Thames motor-driven tug and cargo boat, 184, annotated ?1917

29 LMA, 4467/G/03/002, newspaper cutting from the *Cork Constitution*, 21 July 1902, 2

30 *J S J* 1957, 18

31 LMA, 4467/E/01/003, Marking a record, *Square Mag*, January–March 1921, 14

32 LMA, 4467/E/01/003, *Square Mag*, August 1920, 9

33 LMA, 4467/G/03/003/A, newspaper cutting from *Financial News*, 27 May 1920, 110

34 LMA, 4467/G/03/003/A, newspaper cutting from *Evening News*, 24 February 1920, 140

CHAPTER 6

FOOD IN THE LATE VICTORIAN AND EDWARDIAN HOUSEHOLD

6.1 Crosse and Blackwell and Britain's food manufacturing industry

Crosse and Blackwell's rise during the 19th century mirrors the overall modernisation of Britain's food manufacturing industry and food distribution networks that operated and competed in an increasingly global market. Other familiar names soon joined Crosse and Blackwell. The range of jams and marmalades it offered were added to by the lines made by the grocers, James Robertson (founded 1859 in Paisley, Renfrewshire, Scotland), William P Hartley (founded 1871: with factories at Bootle and then Aintree close to Liverpool; it moved to London in 1901[1]) and Lipton's (1892: based in Bermondsey, London). Crosse and Blackwell's pickles, chutneys and sauces product range found competition from Sharwoods (founded 1889 in London). The retailers which stocked and sold these products also developed; the independent British grocer that dominated the early Victorian shopkeeper's landscape – which sold dry and bulk foods, and offered credit and deliveries to their customers – found themselves increasingly squeezed by the rise of the 'co-ops and multiples' by the Edwardian period,[2] for example Sainsbury's (founded 1869[3]) and Marks and Spencer (founded 1894[4]) with the likes of Lipton's, Home and Colonial Stores and Maypole's Dairy Company between them owning nearly 2000 shops.[5]

Despite the emergence of these noted giant food manufacturers and increase in the multiple retailer outlets to stock their products, by the turn of the 20th century a proportion of Britain's population remained malnourished through poverty and were only able to access largely unpalatable and poor-quality foods. It prompted philanthropist and Quaker B Seebohm Rowntree to publish *Poverty: a study of town life* in 1901,[6] a seminal sociological study on the poor of York (Yorkshire) and the potentially damaging consequences of Britain's poor nutrition were sharply brought into focus when 40% of men who accepted the king's shilling and volunteered for the Boer Wars in South Africa (1880–1 and 1899–1902) were rejected for being physically or medically unfit.[7]

In a period where the importance of food science and nutrition was being increasingly understood but not always incorporated into food manufacturing practices, Crosse and Blackwell nevertheless became embroiled in two controversies particular to Victorian Britain. The first relates to one of the main health concerns of the nation: food adulteration. Here grocers, manufacturers and traders added foreign substances to the food products they sold which in turn added weight and thus increased profits (very little food was packaged and was usually weighed to the customer's specifications[8]). In 1851 Dr Arthur Hassall was commissioned by the *Lancet* to write on the methods and extent of food adulteration. Achieved in part through his examination of the composition of a number of common foods and drinks, he discovered that pickles, bottled vegetables and fruit were cooked in copper pans to make them green and therefore fresh looking, and other poisons were used to colour preserved meat and fish.[9] He named Crosse and Blackwell as one of the many guilty culprits, specifically for producing pickles contaminated with copper sulphate, the result of boiling vinegar in copper vessels.[10] The impact of his report was such that a Parliamentary Select Committee on Adulteration of Food was formed in 1855 and Thomas Blackwell was called for questioning, an event recorded in *The Times*. It was reported by the committee that Crosse and Blackwell had 'acknowledged in a most honourable manner that previous to the appearance of articles in the Lancet they had been in the habit of the practicing the adulteration referred to, but since had discontinued doing so' and 'had been very anxious to assist the inquiry in any way'.[11] Blackwell's appearance and honesty seem to have reduced the negative impact that the firm suffered as a result of being named in Hassall's list.[12] By 1860 the firm, after experimenting with various materials to replace their tainted copper vessels, had settled on steaming jams and jellies in silver pans to evaporate the watery portion of fruit.[13]

Whilst Louis Pasteur's famous theories and methods on the preserving and spoilage of food by destroying bacteria through heat came a few years too late (in 1860) to be taken into account by the Parliamentary Select Committee, throughout the mid to late 19th century Crosse and Blackwell frequently emphasised that their foods were produced 'without even a trace of artificial colouring and are preserved with the best malt vinegar by themselves at their vinegar Brewery in Brewery Road'.[14] However, *The Times* recorded that Thomas's successor, his son Thomas F Blackwell, was called to a Parliamentary Committee some 45 years later. Here he gave evidence to the departmental committee on preservatives and colouring matter in food and confirmed that, whilst preservatives were not standard additions in preserved fruit and jams, Crosse and Blackwell used colouring matter in vegetables and 'used extract of cochineal to attain a uniform colour in their jams'.[15] Makers of jams had yet to use pectin, the substance in fruits that cause jams and jellies to set.[16]

The idea that keeping the putrefying agent of air out of food, first discovered by the French confectioner Nicholas Appert in 1795,[17] was critical to its longevity, and preservation led to an increase in the number of patented containers in pottery and glass that could claim to be airtight. This can be observed in the 1873 published illustrated price lists of the London stoneware manufacturers of Doulton and Watts[18] and James Stiff and Sons[19] (Chapter 4.3) which present various 'covered jars', 'shut-over covered jars' and 'registered air-tight covered jars' specifically made for the food manufacturing industry that would have best sealed food within an airtight environment and prevented deterioration of the contents. Despite these vessels being available, however, the pottery assemblages from Crosse and Blackwell's premises did not present evidence of these being used by the company.

The second controversy for Crosse and Blackwell, but whose impact on the their fortunes is less certain, was the firm's supply of packaged foods to Admiral Franklin's ill-fated and disastrous 1845 Artic expedition to navigate and map the north-west passage through Canada to Asia. The reasons for the failure of the expedition have been keenly debated,[20] in particular since the results of autopsies on the remains of three of the sailors in the 1980s suggested that lead poisoning from the poorly soldered tin cans was responsible for the death of most of the 129 crew of the two ships that took part, HMS *Terror* and *Erebus*.[21] Admiral Franklin's expedition was well furnished and rationed with the 'considerable equipment of Mssrs. Crosse & Blackwell provisions, preserved meat etc',[22] but the expedition's failure and the evidence of cannibalism on the skeletons of the crew found by later search parties deeply shocked Victorian Britain. Whilst the lead poisoning theory was not current at the time, the crew's starvation was attributed to poor rationing and food, and led the compiler of *A bundle of letters* that related to Crosse and Blackwell, published in 1910, to add a footnote to one letter which discusses how the firm had some of the tins from Point Victory, near Cape Victoria (Canada), collected and kept (on 6 May 1859) by the later search party led by 'Lieut. Hobson [who] found a cairn and a tin case and numerous skeletons from Franklin's expedition'. The footnote describes how one of the collected meat tins had been opened at a meeting of the Royal Geographic Society where it was found to be in 'excellent condition',[23] presumably in an attempt to absolve the firm of any blame.

6.2 The First World War: its impact on Crosse and Blackwell

The company immediately responded to the outbreak of hostilities with Germany and the Austro-Hungarian Empire on 4 August 1914 by raising its price list by 10%, temporarily stopping its exports (Fig 69) and having to cope with the immediate loss of almost half its horses to the British Army.[24] Whilst this inevitably led to delays in customer orders, it soon impacted their staffing levels and by December 1914, 99 of the 502 men employed in their Soho premises had volunteered to join Kitchener's army.[25]

Yet the primary concern expressed in a number of the company's records[26] during the 1914–18 war was the problem of obtaining sugar and fruit to maintain its extensive and important preserve line. In peace time Britain drew two thirds of its supplies of sugar from the Austro-Hungarian Empire,[27] with which it was now at war, but there had been considerable problems in the sourcing and pricing of sugar beet in Britain for at least a decade after the British government had signed the trade protection Brussels Sugar Convention with the European powers in 1902, a situation compounded by a series of subsequent sugar beet crop failures in Europe. By 1916, the British government switched its sourcing of sugar to Cuba and America,[28] but the interruption in supplies caused one of Crosse and Blackwell's competitors, Keiller and Sons, to suspend its sales of orange marmalade due to the shortage of pots, oranges and sugar at the beginning of that year.[29] William Hartley summed up the frustrations of the jam and food manufacturing sector well when he wrote in 1916, 'We are short of labour, short of sugar, in a word short of everything'.[30]

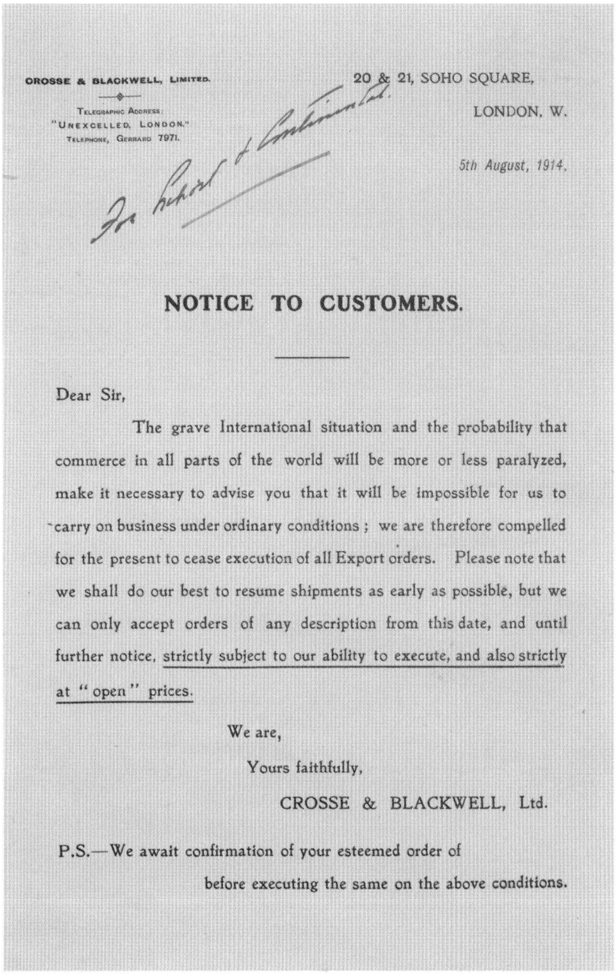
CROSSE & BLACKWELL, LIMITED.
TELEGRAPHIC ADDRESS: "UNEXCELLED, LONDON."
TELEPHONE, GERRARD 7971.

20 & 21, SOHO SQUARE,
LONDON, W.

5th August, 1914.

For Export & Continental

NOTICE TO CUSTOMERS.

Dear Sir,

The grave International situation and the probability that commerce in all parts of the world will be more or less paralyzed, make it necessary to advise you that it will be impossible for us to carry on business under ordinary conditions; we are therefore compelled for the present to cease execution of all Export orders. Please note that we shall do our best to resume shipments as early as possible, but we can only accept orders of any description from this date, and until further notice, strictly subject to our ability to execute, and also strictly at "open" prices.

We are,
Yours faithfully,
CROSSE & BLACKWELL, Ltd.

P.S.—We await confirmation of your esteemed order of
before executing the same on the above conditions.

Fig 69 Letter from Crosse and Blackwell distributed to its customers, dated 5 August 1914, outlining the company's immediate response to the outbreak of the First World War
(LMA, 4467/G/03/002)

The First World War also affected other Crosse and Blackwell product lines. Due to shortages of bottles and closures, the company's pickle orders remained four to five weeks in arrears.[31] By 1917 restrictions on food manufacturers' imports and exports meant it could no longer export 'Pickles, Jams, Huntley & Palmers Biscuits, Meat and Fish'.[32] Fruit and jam prices were fixed by the British government in spring 1917[33] and civilian rationing began on New Year's Day 1918, a result of Germany's successful U-boat campaign of blockading the Atlantic.[34]

Crosse and Blackwell's role in the First World War is articulated in 'A great task how it was tackled', an article written by Miss G I Fowler (MBE) in the *Square Magazine* of July 1920.[35] Upon the outbreak of war, the Admiralty and then the War Office first contacted Keiller to supply a large quantity of preserves for the troops; however, as this was still very much a seasonal product 'This call came at a difficult time for preserve-makers, the soft fruit season being over and most of the supplies sold, the only fruits that were available being mainly plums, damsons and apples'.[36] Victualling a much expanded British army with jams and preserves after the introduction of conscription in January 1916 led Fowler to record the War Office's decision 'to concentrate its buying, and employed eight selected firms for this purpose, our three Companies, of course, being included. The contracts stipulated for joint buying, and it was decided that representatives of the eight firms should regularly meet at Keiller's Offices, at 15 Eastcheap' (in the City of London).[37] Fowler's article goes on to describe how the eight firms faced 'Difficulties of all kinds relating to tins, containers, cases, fruit, labour, and last, but not least, sugar, came up for discussion and solution'.[38]

The impact that the First World War had on food manufacturing and in particular packaging, both during and for years after the conflict had ended, cannot be understated, in particular on the increased use of packets and tins over glass and pots. When they first met (in 1916), the total contracts of the eight firms stood at 2,000,000 tins per week (c 8,000,000lb (3.63 kilotonne) per month if tins assumed to be 1lb as below) but by the height of the war it was 17,000,000lb (7.71 kilotonne) per month,[39] with Crosse and Blackwell's tin shop now making large quantities of 'Ration tins'.[40] The switch from pots to packets for their preserves is also noted with 'the standardised package which was originally in the 1-lb [0.454kg] tin and afterwards the cardboard container could be sent out each week in the quantities required to meet the Government's demands'.[41] By 1920 Fowler suggests that 'a pot of the celebrated Dundee Marmalade, which has never lost and never will lose its charm to the palate' still remained in its war emergency package 'but we shall all feel more satisfied when we see it reigning supreme in its original white pot'.[42]

It appears that whilst Crosse and Blackwell continued to favour ceramics, glass, tins and packets to package its products into the first decade of the 20th century, after the First World War the balance appears to shift away from 'pots' towards glass, packets and tins. Already by 1916, the tin shop was making 4lb [1.81kg] machine-made jam tins for export,[43] presumably as tin was a lighter material for carriage than pots. A way of assessing the change in the containers the company employed during this period can be achieved through comparing the most relevant wholesale price lists that have survived prior to the First World War (for 1910[44]), against the first illustrated export price list of 1923.[45] While tin, glass and packets remained the most frequent and consistent materials used to present their foods in both the 1910 and 1923 lists, differences can be observed between both for a number of the products found on the site. For example, whilst the 1910 price list gives (stoneware) pots as the containers for 'Extractum Carnis'[46] (<P18>–<P22>, Fig 41) and 'Household Jam',[47] by 1923 'Extractum Carnis' is presented in packets,[48] with glass jars or tins reserved for their 'Household Jam'.[49] Another of their important product lines, 'Pure Orange Marmalade'[50] presented in either glass or pots in 1910, was also sold in tins by 1923.[51]

In the years immediately after the First World War the nation plunged into economic recession and the price for commodities remained inflated,[52] but the company appears to have weathered these storms and absorbed high prices. The demand and costs for fruit and sugar in particular remained high in 1919, to the extent that one of Crosse and Blackwell's competitors, Hartley's, ran out of sugar in the summer of that year and forced it to close down production on two of its jam lines.[53] This situation was in part due to a combination of high crop prices and a 'scrambling among individual traders for supplies. In certain cases forward contracts for fruit made by traders were of a speculative character, and tended unduly to raise prices'.[54] This led to the appointment of a Parliamentary subcommittee to discover whether a combine existed among jam manufacturers and if this had any effect on prices. The subcommittee report absolved Crosse and Blackwell of any charges of entering into forward contracts for fruit for a number of years at a fixed price and a *Financial Times* article suggested they had not profiteered from the situation[55] and instead blamed other jam manufacturers and the cooperative societies.

Notes to Chapter 6

1   Hartley 2011

2   Winstanley 1983, 120

3   *J S J* 1993, 18

4   *Marks in time*

5   LMA, 4467/G/03/002, 193, Amazing growth of the multiple shop, 21 November 1913

6   Rowntree 2000

7   Hartley 2011, 24

8   *J S J* 1993, 18

9   Ehrman 1999, 77

10 Atkins 2013, 45

11 *The Times*, Adulteration of food, drinks and drugs, 19 July 1855, 7

12 Atkins 2013, 45

13 LMA, 4467/G/03/002, 162, offprint of *Leisure Hour*, 1860

14 LMA 4467/A/01/003

15 *The Times*, Food preservatives, 20 January 1900, 10

16 Atkins 2013, 50 footnote 46

17 *Nicolas Appert*

18 Green 1999, 365–8

19 Ibid, 361–4

20 Mackie 2014

21 Rowbotham 1987

22 LMA, 4467/A/03/001, 11 footnote 3, letter to brother Chris from his brother George, 5 July 1845

23 LMA, 4467/A/03/001, 16 footnote 3, letter to Reginald, 26 August 1860

24 LMA, 4467/G/03/002, 226

25 LMA, 4467/G/03/002, 233–4, letter from Crosse and Blackwell Ltd to the Secretary of the War Office, 1 December 1914

26 LMA, 4467/G/03/002

27 Tames 2003, 34

28 LMA, 4467/G/03/003, Empire sugar, *Public Ledger*, 7 August 1916

29 LMA, 4467/G/03/002, 277, letter from James Keiller and Son Ltd, 28 January 1916

30 Hartley 2011, 108

31 LMA, 4467/G/03/002, 287, letter from Crosse and Blackwell Ltd, 13 April 1916

32 LMA, 4467/G/03/003, 56, important notice from Crosse and Blackwell Ltd

33 LMA, 4467/E/01/003, A great task how it was tackled, *Square Mag*, July 1920, 9

34 Tames 2003, 35

35 LMA, 4467/E/01/003, A great task how it was tackled, *Square Mag*, July 1920, 7–9

36 LMA, 4467/E/01/003, A great task how it was tackled, *Square Mag*, July 1920, 7

37 LMA, 4467/E/01/003, A great task how it was tackled, *Square Mag*, July 1920, 8

38 LMA, 4467/E/01/003, A great task how it was tackled, *Square Mag*, July 1920, 8

39 LMA, 4467/E/01/003, A great task how it was tackled, *Square Mag*, July 1920, 8

40 LMA, 4467/C/02/002, 110, 115

41 LMA, 4467/E/01/003, A great task how it was tackled, *Square Mag*, July 1920, 8

42 LMA, 4467/E/01/003, A great task how it was tackled, *Square Mag*, July 1920, 9

43 LMA, 4467/C/02/002, May 1916, 105

44 LMA, 4467/D/01/001

45 LMA, 4467/D/01/002

46 LMA, 4467/D/01/001, 5, product no. 25

47 LMA, 4467/D/01/001, 6, product no. 33

48 LMA, 4467/D/01/002, 28, product no. 464

49 LMA, 4467/D/01/002, 17, product no. 278

50 LMA, 4467/D/01/002, 6, product no. 42

51 LMA, 4467/D/01/002, 20, product no. 304

52 LMA, 4467/G/03/003/A, newspaper cutting from *The Times*, 27 May 1920, 108

53 Hartley 2011, 113

54 LMA, 4467/G/03/003/A, 133, newspaper cutting from *Morning Post*, 6 August 1920

55 LMA, 4467/G/03/003/A, 133, newspaper cutting from *Financial Times*, 6 August 1920

CHAPTER 7

CONCLUSION

This book has demonstrated how, from their first premises at 11 King Street with Crosse and Blackwell employing 15 staff in 1845, the retail and food manufacturing landscape by which it operated as the Victorian period progressed changed beyond recognition. The mechanisms by which their food was sold shifted. The market share of the traditional grocer of the first part of the 19th century, who operated on a credit and home delivery system, had, by the Edwardian period, been increasingly eroded by the likes of the multiples of Sainsbury's, Lipton's and Marks and Spencer. The technological improvements in the manufacturing of glass and tins, combined with an increased awareness of the importance of using airtight containers, transformed how foods were stored and how long they could be kept. This, together with steamships and refrigeration now enabled food to be transported and preserved on a global scale.

At the point of Crosse and Blackwell's departure from London for Branston, the net profit for the company for the year that ended 28 February 1921 stood at £592,178.[1] After apparently weathering the effects of the Great War and acquiring companies such as Keiller and Sons as subsidiaries, Crosse and Blackwell's salmon canneries in North America had been added to by expansions in South Africa, Argentina, France and Belgium. They appeared well set for further national and global success. The much vaunted move to Branston, however, proved short-lived. As the result of poor financing, just two years later Crosse and Blackwell had relocated their factory operations back to London, not to their original premises in Soho but to Bermondsey, south London. Here they expanded the Crimscott Street factory they had recently acquired from Lazenby and Sons, premises located close to the factory and warehouse of one of their main competitors, Hartley's. The company nevertheless continued as a British food manufacturing leader in its own right until 1960, when Nestlé acquired a capital share of Crosse and Blackwell.[2]

Whilst a substantive archive for Crosse and Blackwell and many of its acquisitions from 1830 to the 1990s are curated in the London Metropolitan Archive,[3] this can only reflect a small proportion of the total volume of records the company generated. The combination of the standing building surveys and the excavations conducted on their Soho premises, together with extensive archival research, have for the first time provided a unique and unprecedented insight into the infrastructure and material culture of Crosse

Fig 70 'A group of C & B goods': illustration from the *Square Magazine*, 1921

(LMA, 4467/E/01/003, January–March 1921, 9)

and Blackwell's Soho operation, whose products (Fig 70) filled the cupboards of Britain's households and those of others around the globe.

Notes to Chapter 7

1 LMA, 4467/G/03/003/A, newspaper cutting from

2 *The Times*, 14 April 1921
   Our family, our history

3 LMA, 4467; most of

the company's archive is from the 1830s to the first half of the 20th century

BIBLIOGRAPHY

Manuscript sources

City of Westminster Archives Centre, London (CWAC)

Goad insurance map, Charing Cross Road, London vol IX sheet 224–5, 1889

London Metropolitan Archives (LMA)

Records of Crosse and Blackwell Limited consulted as follows:

CORPORATE AGREEMENTS

4467/A/01/001   abstract of articles of the partnership between Edmund Crosse and Thomas Blackwell, dated 31 March 1830

4467/A/01/002   deed of covenant: Crosse and Blackwell with Alexis Soyer, dated 22 August 1853

4467/A/01/003   declaration of the quality of goods: extract of minutes confirming quality of Crosse and Blackwell's produce, with Dutch seal, dated 1874

4467/A/01/004   letter and certificate confirming Crosse and Blackwell as provider of goods to the Ministry of the Home of Emperor Napoleon, dated April 1868

4467/A/01/005   letter granting Crosse and Blackwell right of supplier to the household of the king of Belgium, dated June 1868

CORRESPONDENCE

4467/A/02/005   letter from Victor Crosse to L E Jackson regarding early history of the organisation and royal warrants, dated 1953

4467/G/03/002   letter from Crosse and Blackwell to its customers outlining the company's immediate response to the outbreak of the First World War, dated 5 August 1914

LEDGERS

4467/B/02/001   account notebook, 1830–3

4467/C/02/002   tin shop ledger, dated 1912–20

NEWSPAPER CUTTINGS

4467/G/03/002   cuttings, 1900–16, and various ephemera including earlier dated documents

4467/G/03/003   cuttings, 1916–20, including company internal letters and memos

4467/G/03/003/A   cuttings, 1920–1, and various ephemera including earlier dated documents

PREMISES

4467/F/02/004   'An inventory & valuation of the plant, utensils, fixtures and sundry effects on the premises at Soho Square, Sutton Place, George Yard, Denmark Street, Stacey Street, Dean Street and Earl Street. The property of Messers Crosse and Blackwell, made & taken as on the 1st January 1868'

PRODUCTION AGREEMENTS

4467/C/01/001   assignment of invention with Christopher Dinmore: essence of anchovies, dated 31 January 1853

4467/C/01/002   deed of covenant: Soyer's Aromatic Mustard, dated 19 February 1853

4467/C/01/003   assignment of invention with George Payne: Payne's Royal Osborne Sauce, dated 3 March 1857

4467/C/01/004   deed of covenant: Soyer's Padischa/Sultana Sauce 1 document, dated 3 March 1857

4467/C/01/007   agreement with James Winter regarding patents for filling and corking bottles in vacuum, dated 1 April 1870

PUBLISHED HISTORY

4467/A/03/001   'A bundle of old letters': a narrative history of Crosse and Blackwell, 1910

SALES PRICE LISTS

4467/D/01/001   wholesale price lists, dated 1910

4467/D/01/002   illustrated price list, dated 1923

STAFF ORGANISATIONS AND PUBLICATIONS

4467/E/01/003   Square Mag, 1920–1

4467/E/01/004   Soho Star, 1924

4467/E/01/005   copy of article regarding the history of the company by Victor Crosse, in Group News, 1962

4467/E/01/006   Combine Link newsletter, 26 November 1928: lecture delivered by Frank Blackwell, Esquire, directory at 20 Soho Square, Wednesday, 21 November 1928, 1–11

Printed and other secondary works

About us [Crosse and Blackwell]   Crosse & Blackwell: about us, http://www.crosseandblackwell.com/about (last accessed 10 June 2015)

Acton, E, 1845   Modern cookery, in all its branches: reduced to a system of easy practice, for the use of private families, London

Advert for Gordon and Dilworth   British Library online gallery: advert for Gordon and Dilworth's tomato catsup, http://www.bl.uk/onlinegallery/onlineex/evancoll/a/014eva000000000u04172000.html (last accessed 15 July 2015)

Askey, D, 1998 (1981)   Stoneware bottles, 1500–1949, 2 updated edn, Brighton

Atkins, P, 2013   Vinegar and sugar: the early history of factory-made jams, pickles and sauces in Britain, in The food industries of Europe in the 19th and 20th centuries (eds D J Oddy and A Drouard), 41–54, Farnham (consulted at http://www.academia.edu/3550965/Vinegar_and_sugar_the_early_history_of_factory-made_jams_pickles_and_sauces_in_Britain, last accessed 8 June 2015)

Becker, K, 2014   Conservation report [TCG09], unpub MOLA rep

Blackmore, L, 2014   The accessioned finds and related bulk items (excluding glass, clay tobacco pipes and building materials) [TCG09], unpub MOLA rep

Blackmore, L, and Jeffries, N, 2014   The post-medieval bulk and accessioned glass [TCG09], unpub MOLA rep

Board of Works for the St Giles District, 1871   *The report of the Medical Officer of Health for 1870*, London (consulted at http://wellcomelibrary.org/moh/, last accessed 28 July 2014)

Bottle closures   Bottle finishes and closures: Part 3, Types of bottle closures, http://www.sha.org/bottle/closures.htm#Glass (last accessed 10 June 2015)

Bowsher, J, 2014   C261 archaeology early east: post-excavation assessment and updated research design, TCR East (TCG09), unpub MOLA rep

Bryan Donkin   Canmaker: Bryan Donkin, the world's first canmaker, 10 September 2013, http://www.canmaker.com/news/feature-articles/2624-bryan-donkin-the-worlds-first-canmaker (last accessed 25 May 2014)

Builder, 1877   R L Roumieu [obituary], *Builder* 35 (7 July), 691

Cherry, B, and Pevsner, N, 1998   *London: Vol 4, North*, London

Copeland, R, 1990 (1980)   *Spode's willow pattern and other designs after the Chinese*, 2 edn, London

Creswick, A, 1987   *The fruit jar works: Vol 1, Listing jars made c 1820 to 1920s*, Grand Rapids

Crosse and Blackwell   http://www.crosseandblackwell.co.uk/ (last accessed 10 June 2015)

Docio, A, 2013   History of Worcestershire Sauce, britishlocalfood.com (last accessed 10 June 2015)

Ehrman, E, 1999   19th century, in Ehrman, E, Forsyth, H, Peltz, L and Ross, C, *London eats out: 500 years of capital dining*, 69–85, London

Glassmaking   Historic glass bottle identification and information website: glassmaking and glassmakers, www.sha.org/bottle/glassmaking.htm (last accessed 10 June 2015)

GLIAS, 1984   Greater London Industrial Archaeological Society: notes and news – GLIAS 16th Annual General Meeting, June 1984, http://www.glias.org.uk/news/092news.html (last accessed 18 June 2014)

Grant, I F, 1922   The survival of the small unit in industry, *Econ J* 128, 489–505

Green, C, 1999   *Fulham pottery: excavations 1971–9*, London

Harben, H A, 1918   *Dictionary of London*, London

Hartley, N, 2011   *Bittersweet: the story of Hartley's jam*, Stroud

ILN   Illustrated London News (consulted online at the British Library)

Jeffries, N, 2014   Victorian and later pottery [TCG09], unpub MOLA rep

Jones, F, 1997 (1987)   *Historic Carmarthenshire homes and their families*, 2 edn, Newport

J S J, 1957   Food for history, *J S J* (February), 12–19 (consulted at https://jsjournals.websds.net/, last accessed 10 June 2015)

J S J, 1961   Rations for ratings, *J S J* (June), 19–21 (consulted at https://jsjournals.websds.net/, last accessed 10 June 2015)

J S J, 1993   Archives: how packaging became part of the service, *J S J* (May), 18–19

(consulted at https://jsjournals.websds.net/, last accessed 10 June 2015)

Keogh, B, 1997   *The secret sauce: a history of Lea and Perrins*, no place

Lea & Perrins   Lea & Perrins: the history of Lea & Perrins, http://www.heinz.com/ data/pdf/LeaPerrinsTimeline.pdf (last accessed 17 July 2015)

Lockhart, B, Schreiver, B, Lindsey, B, and Serr, C, nd   Cannington, Shaw and Co, 51–64, http://www.sha.org/bottle/pdffiles/CS%26Co.pdf (last accessed 10 June 2015)

Mackie, R, 2014   Why our explanation of 1845 polar tragedy should be put on ice, *Observer*, 26 January (consulted at http://www.theguardian.com/science/2014/jan/26/ lead-poisoning-polar-sir-john-franklin, last accessed 25 June 2014)

Maling history   Maling Collectors Society: Maling history, http://www.maling-pottery. org.uk/history_c.html (last accessed 10 June 2015)

Marks in time   Marks and Spencer company archive: marks in time, https:// marksintime.marksandspencer.com/home (last accessed 10 June 2015)

Mathew, B, 2000   The Keiller connection, *Maling Collectors' Soc Newslett* 8 (September), 6–7 (consulted at http://www.maling-pottery.org.uk/08.pdf, last accessed 10 June 2015)

Mayhew, H, 1865   The establishment of Messrs Crosse and Blackwell, sauce and pickle manufacturers, in *The shops and companies of London* (ed H Mayhew), 174–88, London

Morgan, W, 1682   'London &c Actually Surveyed', reproduced in Margary, H, 1977 *'London &c Actually Surveyed' by William Morgan, 1682,* Margary in assoc Guildhall Library, Kent

Nicolas Appert   Encyclopaedia Britannica: Nicolas Appert (consulted at www.britannica. com/EBchecked/topic/30573, last accessed 10 June 2015)

Our brands   Mizkan: our brands, http://www.mizkan.co.uk/our-brands/ (last accessed 10 June 2015)

Our family, our history   Crosse & Blackwell: our family, our history, http://www. crosseandblackwell.co.uk/our-family/history/ (last accessed 16 July 2015)

Post Office, 1857   *Post Office London directory 1857*, London

Post Office, 1965   *Post Office London directory 1965*, London

Post Office, 1969   *Post Office London directory 1969*, London

Preserves   Cook's info: preserves, www.cooksinfo.com (last accessed 10 June 2015)

Rocque, J, 1746   'A Plan of the Cities of London Westminster and Southwark with contiguous buildings from an actual survey' by John Rocque, reproduced in Margary, H (ed), 1971 *'An Exact Survey of the City's of London Westminster ye Borough of Southwark and the Country near 10 Miles Round London' [and] 'A Plan of the Cities of London and Westminster and Borough of Southwark with the Contiguous Buildings from an Actual Survey' by John Rocque in 1746,* Margary in assoc Guildhall Library, Kent

Rowbotham, S, 1987   Canned food sealed iceman's fate, *Hist Today* 37(10) (consulted at http://www.historytoday.com/sheila-rowbotham/canned-food-sealed-icemens-fate, last accessed 25 June 2014)

Rowntree, B S, 2000 (1901)   *Poverty: a study of town life*, spec centenary edn, Bristol

Sheppard, F H W (gen ed), 1966   *Survey of London: Vols 33–4, The parish of St Anne, Soho*, London (consulted at http://www.british-history.ac.uk/report.aspx?compid=41110, last accessed 25 May 2014)

Shurtleff, W, and Akiko, A (comps), 2012   *History of Worcestershire Sauce (1837–2012): extensively annotated bibliography and sourcebook*, Lafayette (consulted at http://www.soyinfocenter.com/pdf/152/Worc.pdf, last accessed 16 July 2015)

Sorapure, D, 2010   Crossrail Eastern Ticket Hall, 12 Sutton Row–12 Goslett Yard, London WC2, a standing building report, unpub MOL rep

Sorapure, D, and Karim, A, 2014   The Mossbourne Victoria Park Academy, formerly the French hospital: standing building survey report, unpub MOLA rep

Sorapure, D, and Tetreau, M, 2011   A return to Crystal Palace Station, *London Archaeol* 12, 306–11

South Lanarkshire [RG.1978.485.a]   South Larnarkshire leisure and culture, http://www.sllcmuseumscollections.co.uk/ (last accessed 15 July 2015)

Tames, R, 2003   *Feeding London*, London

The Times   *Times Digital Archive, 1785–2006*, Gale Cengage Learning, gale.cengage.co.uk (last accessed 1 May 2014)

Valenze, D, 2011   *Milk: a local and global history*, Yale

Westman, A, 2009   Tottenham Court Road Station upgrade: 1–15 Oxford Street, 157–167 and 138–148 Charing Cross Road, 1–6 Falconberg Court, standing building survey, unpub MOL rep

Winstanley, M J, 1983   *The shopkeeper's world, 1830–1914*, Manchester

Worcester   Foods of England project: Worcester (or Worcestershire) Sauce, http://foodsofengland.co.uk/worcesterorworcestershiresauce.htm (last accessed 10 June 2015)